Effective Literacy
Instruction

Effective Literacy Instruction

Building Successful
Reading and Writing Programs

Judith A. Langer
The National Research Center on English Learning & Achievement
University at Albany, State University of New York

National Council of Teachers of English
1111 W. Kenyon Road, Urbana, Illinois 61801-1096

Staff Editor: Tom Tiller
Interior Design: Doug Burnett
Cover Design: Pat Mayer

NCTE Stock Number: 12943-3050

It is the policy of NCTE in its journals and other publications to provide a forum for the open discussion of ideas concerning the content and the teaching of English and the language arts. Publicity accorded to any particular point of view does not imply endorsement by the Executive Committee, the Board of Directors, or the membership at large, except in announcements of policy, where such endorsement is clearly specified.

Library of Congress Cataloging-in-Publication Data

Langer, Judith A.
   Effective literacy instruction : building successful reading and writing programs / Judith A. Langer.
         p.   cm.
Includes bibliographical references (p.   ) and index.
   ISBN 0-8141-1294-3 (pbk.)
   1. English language--Study and teaching (Secondary)--United States.
2. Language arts (Secondary)--United States.   I. Title: Building successful reading and writing programs. II. Title.
   LB1631 .L22 2002
   428.4'071'2--dc21

                                                                2002004608

To the districts, the schools, and especially the teachers
who bared their professional lives for us to study and learn from.

To the CELA staff, who were there at every moment needed.

J. A. L.

Contents

1 Effective Literacy Programs

"Effective." You will encounter that term throughout this book. You'll read about effective teachers, effective instruction, effective English programs. So right away, I want to clarify what I mean by "effective." It's really quite simple. The students of the English teachers you'll be meeting in this book become truly literate, in the highest sense of the word. The teachers work within the realities of modern-day middle school and high school English classrooms, most in poor, urban areas with minority students. When you walk into these teachers' classrooms, you sense immediately that something special is going on. You see and hear students engaged with literature, practiced in writing, comfortable with intelligent literary discourse. The students are learning to write, talk about, and extract meaning from knowledge and experience in the ways that school, work, and life demand in the twenty-first century. These are effective teachers.

This book, like the study that prompted it, is not only about effective teachers. It's also about the kind of effective English programs that foster and sustain effective teachers. It's based on a five-year study I directed at the National Research Center on English Learning & Achievement (CELA). The study, which we called the Excellence in English (EIE) project, provided answers to two primary questions: (1) What kind of English instruction is enabling students to develop the kinds of literacy needed in the twenty-first century? and (2) What kind of programs are enabling these teachers to instruct so effectively? You'll be reading my answers to these questions in the next two chapters. Chapters 4 through 7 provide a more in-depth look at particularly effective teachers and programs. These chapters include the work of some of the field researchers who helped me study middle school and high school language arts programs. In all, they were Paola Bonissone, Carla Confer, Gladys Cruz, Ester Helmar-Salasoo, Sally Jo Bronner, Tanya Manning, Steven Ostrowski, Eija Rougle, and Anita Stevens. I hope that, together, the chapters will help English professionals imagine what might be done to infuse programs with the features that have been shown to make a difference in English language learning.

Excellence in English was undertaken during a time (that still continues) when English teachers were feeling extreme pressure regarding student performance on high-stakes tests. In an attempt to be helpful to the field, I sought to learn more about what was happening in schools that were doing better than comparable schools not only in classwork but also on high-stakes tests. I did not (and do not) condone the way tests are being used in some localities, nor did the teachers we studied necessarily condone them. However, high-stakes tests were part of these teachers' realities, and I wanted the study to help them help their students perform well, without selling out. I wanted to see how schools that were hardworking and professional were going about things in an era of high-stakes testing—and doing comparatively better, or not, in terms of the tests. Lots of my colleagues were arguing for or against the benefits of today's high-stakes emphasis. I felt a productive route for me and my research team was to see if we could learn something useful about how effective schools were handling the realities. The findings, as the following chapters describe, are quite revealing. That is, in higher-performing schools, high-stakes tests do not dominate the curriculum, and the best of English professionalism carries the day. Details follow. In the remainder of this chapter, I will describe the study. All else will provide detail of the features that make the difference. My hope is that this book will be used to help teachers reclaim their professionalism while helping their students become more highly literate.

The Excellence in English Project

The study focused on the educational practices that support high literacy. By "high literacy" I mean much more than reading simple texts with superficial understanding or writing in a manner that is merely comprehensible. English classrooms have long been considered places where high literacy (Bereiter & Scardamalia, 1987) is learned, where students gain not merely the basic literacy skills to get by, but also the content knowledge, ways of structuring ideas, and ways of communicating with others that are considered the "marks" of an educated person (Graff, 1987). Certainly basic reading and writing skills are included in what I refer to as high literacy. Yet it also includes the ability to use language, content, and reasoning in ways that are appropriate for particular situations and disciplines. Students learn to "read" the social meanings, the rules and structures, and the linguistic and cognitive routines to make things work in the real world of English language use. That knowledge becomes available as options when they confront new situations. This notion of high literacy refers to a deeper knowledge of the ways in which reading, writing, language, and content work together. This kind of literacy, I believe, belongs at the heart of the teaching and learning of English across the grades. It is reflected in students' abilities to: engage in thoughtful reading, writing, and discussion in the classroom; use their knowledge and skills in new situations; and perform well on a wide variety of reading and writing tasks, including high-stakes tests.

In today's public and educational arenas, concerns focus not merely on test scores but on approaches to curriculum and instruction, the teaching of skills and knowledge, and the professional as well as the classroom contexts that support them: basic problems of practice that have been the focus of previous waves of reform. The problems become particularly acute at times when schools are called upon to reform their programs, since effective reform requires a clear vision of the kinds of learning that are sought and the approaches that are most likely to achieve them. The lack of such a vision is one of the central problems English educators (indeed, all educators) are facing today. Reforms compete with one another for attention, and professionals are faced with changing views of appropriate goals in a changing society (Myers, 1996). Yet amidst the debates, many districts and teachers are already educating their students very successfully, providing an environment that supports the development of high literacy for diverse populations.

You'll be reading about some of these districts and teachers in the chapters that follow. We chose them for our study, and for this book, based on a combination of recommendations and test scores. First, we limited our study to four states: California, Florida, New York, and Texas. Then, we asked educators from state education departments, the National Council of Teachers of English (NCTE), and other national, state, and local organizations and groups, as well as teachers and administrators, to recommend schools and teachers who had a reputation for excellence in English, who were trying hard to offer excellent instruction and also raise scores. After receiving recommendations, we checked the Internet for state data on test scores. We learned that some of the schools' scores were higher than comparable schools with similar demographics, while others were typical, scoring similarly to those with comparable populations. We focused on schools whose students were "beating the odds," that is, scoring higher on high-stakes tests than students in demographically comparable schools. We made a final selection based on the teachers' and administrators' willingness to work with us over a two-year period, as well as the school's ability to contribute to the overall diversity in student populations, problems, and locations in our sample.

In the end, we selected twenty-five schools and forty-four teachers. We studied eighty-eight classes—one class for each of the teachers in each of two consecutive years. Of the twenty-five participating schools, fourteen were places where students were beating the odds: Students were engaged in learning and were thinking, writing, and conversing about the literature they were reading. In addition, they were performing better on state-administered reading and writing tests than were students at schools rated as comparable by state criteria. The other eleven schools were places where administrators were concerned and most individual teachers were trying hard to have their students learn, but student achievement—in classroom activities and on standardized tests—was typical of other schools with similar demographics. The level of student engagement and development of high literacy was significantly lower in these schools. As Table 1 depicts, the twenty-five schools represent a wide range of economic and cultural communities.[1]

Types of Schools

In Florida, we studied schools from the Miami-Dade County area, representing a very diverse student population. The Miami-Dade County School District has long been involved in cutting-edge efforts to improve education in English, including in part: Pacesetter (sponsored by the College Board), the Zelda Glazer/Dade County Writing Project, the instruction of all teachers in the education of nonnative English-speaking students, the creation of interdisciplinary teams, and the early development of school-based management. (Chapter 4 focuses on Miami-Dade County.)

In New York, we covered a large geographic area, with populations ranging from rural to urban and crossing all socioeconomic lines. This included a number of districts in New York City and the Hudson Valley region that have earned reputations for student-centered and response-based English education, an emphasis on writing and reading across the curriculum, implementation of Goals 2000 initiatives, and an interdisciplinary approach to math, science, and real-world studies through the English language arts. Two programs we studied—at King Middle School and International High School—focus on high academic competence for English Language Learners (ELL) students. (Chapter 5 describes the International program, and Chapter 6 focuses on a school upstate.)

Table 1. School Demographics

School	Student membership	Free or reduced lunch	Selected features	Teacher	Category‡
Florida					
+Highland Oaks M.S.*	47% White 27% Hispanic 23% African American	34%	interdisciplinary teams; academic wheels; collaborative partnerships	Rita Gold Susan Gropper	1 1
Ruben Dario M.S.*	83% Hispanic 12% African American 4% White	80%	team and decision-making councils; reading and language arts across areas	Karis MacDonnell Gail Slatko	1 1
+Wm. H. Turner Tech. Arts H.S.*	63% African American 33% Hispanic 4% White	45%	dual academic and work-related academies; workplace experience; Coalition of Essential Schools	Chris Kirchner Janas Masztal	1 1
Hendricks H.S.	56% Hispanic 43% African American	47%	International Business and Finance Magnet; Jr. ROTC; dropout prevention	Elba Rosales Carol McGuinness	2 3
Miami Edison H.S.*	92% African American 8% Hispanic	38%	new academies; teams; writing and English in subject areas	Shawn DeNight Kathy Humphrey	2 2
Palm M.S.	60% African American 39% Hispanic 1% White	85%	Arts Magnet; tracking; interdisciplinary teams	Nessa Jones	3

continued

Table 1 (cont.). School Demographics

School	Student membership	Free or reduced lunch	Selected features	Teacher	Category
New York					
⁺King M.S.	43% White 33% Hispanic 21% African American	40%	interdisciplinary teams; active departments; dual language	Pedro Méndez Donald Silvers	1 1
⁺Hudson M.S.	92% White 4% African American	5%	interdisciplinary teams; active departments	Cathy Starr Gloria Rosso	1 1
⁺International H.S.*	48 countries 37 languages	84%	academic teams; internships; portfolios; exhibitions	Marsha Slater Aaron Listhaus	1 1
Crestwood M.S.	66% White 25% African American 5% Asian 4% Hispanic	62%	interdisciplinary teams; departments	Monica Matthews	3
New Westford H.S.	68% White 22% African American 6% Hispanic 4% Asian	36%	departments; grade-level teams; arts focus	Elaine Dinardi Jack Foley	3 3
Stockton M.S.	62% White 23% African American 14% Hispanic 1% Asian	46%	interdisciplinary teams; departments	Helen Ross	3
Tawasentha H.S.	97% White	12%	curriculum teams; facilitators	Margaret Weiss Nicole Scott	2 3

continued

7

Table 1 (cont.). School Demographics

School	Student membership	Free or reduced lunch	Selected features	Teacher	Category
California					
+Charles Drew M.S.	55% Hispanic 32% White 8% African American 4% Asian	57%	literacy coaching; Strategic Reading Program	Alicia Alliston Tawanda Richardson	1 1
James A. Foshay Learning Center +Foshay M.S.** +Foshay H.S.**	69% Hispanic 31% African American	86%	USC precollege program; New American School; Urban Learning Center; academies	Kate McFadden-Midby Myra LeBendig	1 1
+Springfield H.S.	63% Hispanic 15% White 10% African American 9% Asian	26%	Foreign Language/International Studies Magnet; UCLA collaborative; Career Ed; Bilingual Business/Finance Academy	Celeste Rotondi Suzanna Matton	1 1
Rita Dove M.S.	58% Hispanic 41% African American	72%	literacy coaching; health/science career magnet; districtwide reform initiative	Jonathan Luther Evangeline Turner	3 2
Rutherford Hayes H.S.	86 % Hispanic 7% Asian 3% Filipino 2% White 2% African American	74%	Humanitas program; teams; Math/Science Magnet; service learning	Ron Soja	3

continued

Table 1 (cont.). School Demographics

School	Student membership	Free or reduced lunch	Selected features	Teacher	Category
Texas					
+John H. Kirby M.S.	42% White 34% Hispanic 17% African American 7% Asian	32%	Annenberg Beacon Charter School; Vanguard Magnet; Pre-International Baccalaureate Program; school-based center for teacher development; special program for low-motivated students; reading and language arts double dose for 6th grade; interdisciplinary teams	Cynthia Spencer-Bell Matt Caldwell	1 1
+Lincoln H.S.	78% African American 18% Hispanic 2% White 1% Asian	41%	Active English department; Aviation Sciences Magnet; Navy ROTC; Language Arts Consortium with Ruby M.S.	Viola Collins Vanessa Justice	1 1
+Lyndon B. Johnson H.S.	53% Hispanic 23% White 21% African American 2% Asian	37%	Research & Technology Magnet; International Baccalaureate Program; ROTC; departments; grade level teams	Thelma Moore Nora Shepherd	1 1
+Parklane M.S.	47% Hispanic 38% White 13% African American 3% Asian	46%	Active English Department; Reading and Language Arts (double dose)	Rachel Kahn Amy Julien	1 1

continued

Table 1 (cont.). School Demographics

School	Student membership	Free or reduced lunch	Selected features	Teacher	Category
Texas (cont.)					
Ruby M.S.	83% African American 15% Hispanic 2% White	67%	English Department; Reading and Language Arts (double dose); Language Arts Consortium with Lincoln H.S.	Shaney Young Erica Walker	3 3
Sam Rayburn H.S.	87% Hispanic 7% African American 5% White 1% Asian	58%	Computer Technology Magnet; extensive vocational education program; ROTC; double English in grades 9 and 10; departments; Annenberg Challenge Reform Initiative	Carol Lussier Jo Beth Chapin	2 3

‡ In the Category column, 1 denotes effective teacher in effective school; 2 denotes effective teacher in typically performing school; 3 denotes typical teacher in typically performing school.

⁺ Denotes schools whose scores on state assessments were above those of demographically comparable schools.

* Denotes participants' preference to use real names. In such cases, the actual names of schools, project teachers, and their colleagues are used. For the schools not marked with an asterisk, pseudonyms are used throughout this book.

** We studied both the middle school and high school programs at Foshay Learning Center.

In California, we studied schools from the Los Angeles area, another region with a very diverse student population which has long been a bellwether for educational innovation and change in English language arts designed to benefit all students. Most recently, in an effort to raise student performance on statewide assessments, the following efforts have been put into place: a new curriculum, an end to social promotion, a requirement for schools to adopt one of several reform programs, school accountability for student achievement (with schools placed on probation for failure to increase scores), and extra funds for tutoring efforts.

The Texas schools were located in a large city district. Both the state and the district have been involved in major efforts to improve student performance in literacy achievement, including an end to social promotion and a stringent school accountability program to monitor achievement. The district put into place several measures to support improved instruction, and the state assessments were being revised at the time of our study. The field researchers each studied one or more programs for two years; hence we were able to study instructional concerns, plans, and enactments over time, with two sets of students. Each researcher spent approximately five weeks per year at each site, including a week at the beginning of the year to interview district personnel, teachers, and students about their goals, plans, and perceptions. This was followed by two weeks per semester to observe classes, to conduct informal interviews, and to shadow the teachers in their professional encounters (e.g., team, department, building, and district meetings). We set up e-mail accounts or spoke by phone or in person in order to maintain weekly contact with teachers and students to discuss classroom and professional experiences. Portfolios were also maintained, and student work mailed weekly, for use in the discussions.

During this time, we came to understand the extent to which the teachers were affected by the larger context in terms of professional growth or malaise, or were achieving unusually good results in spite of the context in which they worked. This led us, eventually, to recognize three broad but distinct patterns within our sample of teachers:

1. effective teachers whose work was sustained, perhaps even created, by the supportive district and/or school context;

2. effective teachers in typical schools who achieved their success due to professional contexts unrelated to the school and/or district (often through participation in professional organizations, such as local affiliates of NCTE, the International Reading Association, or writing projects, or through collaboration with local colleges and universities); and

3. teachers who were more typical, who were dedicated to their students but working within a system of traditions and expectations that did not lift them beyond the accomplishments of other schools with comparable student bodies.

In working with the first category of teachers—effective teachers in schools where students were beating the odds—we found that these unusual teachers were *not* unusual within the contexts in which they worked; that is, their school and/or district (often both) encouraged all teachers, not just those in our study, to achieve comparable professional goals, and our observations of department meetings and our interviews with supervisors and administrators suggested that the instructional approaches of the teachers in our study were widely accepted and carried out in their schools.

In working with the second category of teachers—effective teachers in typical schools—we found that they did not carry out their jobs in programs that provided students and teachers with consistent and strong curriculum and instructional approaches and development. Thus, while their students may have performed better than those in other classes in the school, there was no consistent and strong support that sustained student achievement beyond their individual classrooms.

We found the third category of teachers—typical teachers in typical schools—in departments and schools that did not support their individual growth and that lacked collective consensus about the most effective approaches to educating their particular student body. Refer back to Table 1 for a quick summary of the schools and teachers in the study.

We got to know the people and the programs very well. Although there were excellent teachers in many of the schools we studied, not all schools were performing equally well. And our study indicates that the teacher cannot do it alone—the program makes a difference. The compounded, coordinated, and connected experiences over time and across classes are key contributors to both a higher-caliber learning experience and higher test scores. An excellent teacher without a well-coordinated program can do only so much. In these situations, even the best of teachers can offer students only isolated moments of engrossed learning and rich experience in an otherwise disconnected series of classes.

Although the programs and experiences were different from school to school, we were able to identify, and came to deeply appreciate, particular features of both the instruction and the professional lives of teachers that marked the effective schools. In the next two chapters, I will discuss these features, giving specific examples from the schools we studied.[2]

2 Effective English Instruction in Middle School and High School

This chapter focuses on the features of effectiveness that involve instruction. Because they reach to the heart of instructional beliefs, decisions, and actions, these features take us into the middle of some of the current debates about the nature of effective literacy instruction.

In each of the six sections below, I discuss an issue that is a problem within the field of English language arts instruction, then I relate one of the study's findings about instruction to it and discuss it, providing examples from the schools we studied, both effective and typical. These six issues have been contested in the field, and although we did not begin or carry out our study intending to focus on these issues, they emerged as central to our findings, and it is, I believe, important for them to be considered by English and literacy educators. The issues are: approaches to skills instruction, test preparation, connecting learnings, enabling strategies, conceptions of learning, and classroom organization.

Approaches to Skills Instruction

Throughout at least the twentieth century, there has been an ongoing debate about the manner in which instruction is offered, with some scholars stressing the effectiveness of skills and concept learning through experience-based instruction (e.g., Dewey, 1938) and others stressing mastery of concepts and skills through decontextualized practice (e.g., Bloom, 1971). This has led to a pedagogical side-taking that continues today. For example, Hirsch (1996) calls for students to remember culturally potent facts. A body of genre theorists (see Cope & Kalantzis, 1993) calls for teaching students the rules of organization underlying written forms. Goodman and Wilde (1992) and Graves (1983) call for teaching skills and knowledge within the context of authentic literacy activities. Yet, in a review of studies of instructional practice across the century, Richard Allington and I (Langer & Allington, 1992) found that teachers tend to blur distinctions, using what may appear to theorists as a fusion of theoretically dissimilar approaches.

While this blending of instructional approaches was apparent in all of the classes in the Excellence in English study, the ways in which teachers orchestrated the approaches differed considerably. Across all sites, the instructional approaches followed three patterns that we have termed *separated*, *simulated*, and *integrated*, with different amounts and orchestrations of each in the effective and typical schools.

Separated instruction is what most educators would consider to be direct instruction of isolated skills and knowledge. It often takes place separately from the context of a larger activity, primarily as an introduction, practice, or review. It can be recognized when the teacher tells students particular rules, conventions, or facts, or when instructional material focuses on listings of vocabulary, spelling, or rules. Sometimes this instruction is used as a way to "cover" the curriculum, other times as a way to help students understand and remember underlying conventions and learn how to apply them. Teachers use the separated activity as a way to highlight a particular skill, item, or rule. It is presented in a lesson that is generally not connected to what is occurring before or after it in class—for example, when a teacher puts the distinctive features of a persuasive essay on the board and has the students discuss and try to remember them, perhaps by copying them into their language logs. It occurs when a set of roots are identified and defined. Separated instruction is the teachers' way of drawing the students' attention to a skill, rule, or item of knowledge available for use in the language and literacy activities in which they engage. It is a lesson, exercise, or drill apart in time from larger units of meaning or use.

In comparison, *simulated* instruction involves the application of those concepts and rules within a targeted unit of reading, writing, or oral language. These are often exercises prepared by the teacher or found in packaged teaching materials, in which students are expected to read or write short units of text with the primary purpose of practicing the skill or concept of focus. Previous reading, writing, and oral language work that the students have done is often referred to during discussion of how that skill works in a larger activity and what difference it makes in the quality of the presentation. Often students are asked to find examples of that skill in use in their literature and writing books, as well as in out-of-school activities. They sometimes practice it within the confines of small and limited tasks. I call it *simulated* because the tasks themselves are specially developed for the purpose of practice.

Integrated instruction takes place when students are expected to use their skills and knowledge within the embedded context of a large and purposeful activity, such as writing a letter, report, poem, or play for a particular goal (not merely to practice the skill), or planning, researching, writing, and editing a class newspaper. Here, the focus is on completing a project or activity well, with primary focus on the effectiveness of the work in light of its purpose. This is the time when the skill or knowledge is put to real use as a contributing factor in the success of the work. This becomes a time when the teacher might remind the students of a rule they learned during separated or simulated activities and how it might be useful in the completion of the activity at hand. If extra help is needed, it is provided by other students or by the teacher.

Thus, *separated*, *simulated*, and *integrated* activities all can occur when needed within the ongoing instructional program. Separated and simulated activities serve as ways for students and teachers to "mark" the skill or item of knowledge for future use, while an integrated activity serves as useful application of a marked skill. Of course, a skill can become marked even during an integrated activity. Each approach serves its own function, but together they insure the students' growing control of the skills and knowledge that underlie efficient language and literacy use.

Findings from our study indicate that these three kinds of instruction—separated, simulated, and integrated—are orchestrated differently in the effective as compared to typical schools:

Finding 1

In effective schools, learning and instruction related to knowledge and conventions of English and high literacy take place as separated, simulated, *and* integrated experiences. In contrast, in typical schools, although each approach might be used at some time, one or another instructional approach dominates.

Two-thirds or more of the effective teachers in both effective and typical schools used all three approaches. In comparison, only 17 percent of the typical teachers in typical schools used all three approaches. While 50 percent of the typical teachers used separated skills instruction as their dominant approach, none of the effective teachers did so. Analyses indicate that either the effective teachers used all three approaches with equal focus, or they used separated and simulated approaches but focused on integration a bit more (see Appendix C, Table 1).

For example, Gail Slatko and Karis MacDonnell, effective teachers at an effective school (Ruben Dario Middle School), had students check each other's grammar even when they didn't do peer revision. They, like most of the teachers in the effective schools, also engaged in direct teaching of grammar and usage (e.g., sentence structure, punctuation), and used these lessons as models for their students to rely on when responding to each other's as well as their own work.

MacDonnell used specific strategies to empower her students to be better writers, editors, graphic artists, and publishers. Chris Kirchner at Turner Tech (see Chapter 4) was masterful at scaffolding her students' efforts to interpret the texts they read without sacrificing their learning of literary devices and other features; she used students' own writing as a jumping-off place for inspecting how language works. The teachers also used the literature that students read as models for targeted conventions, language choices, literary concepts, and stylistic devices and made reverberating connections across activities. Grammar and conventions weren't ignored: direct connections, reminders, and instruction were always present.

At Springfield High School, another effective school, Celeste Rotondi and Suzanna Matton, both teachers who embedded skills and mechanics in long-range activities, always exposed their students to separated and simulated as well as integrated experiences and continually monitored their students' acquisition of new skills as well as noting where special help was needed. To help her students learn language and comprehension skills, Rotondi selected difficult vocabulary words out of context and showed her students how those words could be used in class. She often did this as a simulated activity, in the context of the book students were reading, or incorporated it into their writing practice. Using both separated and simulated lessons, she also helped her students learn to justify their answers, summarize information, and make connections. However, these new learnings were continually expected to be applied during integrated activities, such as literature circles.

Matton's literature circle activities also called for students to use the skills and knowledge they were learning. For example, in one instance her students were divided into literature discussion groups and assigned the following roles that changed each week: discussion director, literary luminary, vocabulary enricher, summarizer, and connector. Each student took responsibility for enriching the group discussion from the vantage point of the assigned role. Since these groups continued throughout the year, each student had many opportunities to practice the skills in context, and to see them modeled by the other students. When Matton saw that extra help was needed, she either helped the individual or offered a separated or simulated activity to several students or the entire class, depending on the need.

In comparison, one teacher at Hayes High School, a typical school, responded to the call for greater emphasis on grammar by raiding the book room for a classroom set of *Warriner's English Grammar and Composition*. She said:

> Well, this is how I do it [holding up the book]. I work hard and have no time to read professional journals. I teach five periods and mark papers. I know I have to teach grammar. My students didn't get it before, so I have to teach it. So I use this [*Warriner's*] because it lays out the lessons, and my students can also use it as a reference.

Her skills lessons, through *Warriner's*, were primarily out of context, separate from the rest of her teaching.

Like the Hayes teacher, Carol McGuinness at Hendricks tended to maintain her old ways of teaching vocabulary, using a vocabulary workbook in which students did periodic assignments in parsing words to get at Latin and Greek roots. Although she saw this as giving them a tool for encountering new words, a tool to learn how to learn, it was primarily a separated activity, and we saw no evidence that she had students use these root-word skills elsewhere.

Because Ron Soja taught in the Humanitas program at Hayes, which integrated social studies and contemporary English, he followed the themes called for by that program, and engaged his students in much reading and writing. However, he did not use these as a way to offer or make links among separated, simulated, and integrated experiences. Instead, the skills and knowledge were used primarily within the context of the themed activities, with little direct attention to helping students focus on the development of their underlying literacy knowledge and skills.

Thus, while teachers in the effective schools used a number of well-orchestrated approaches to provide instruction, practice, and use of new learnings in ways that suffused the students' English experiences, those in the typical schools called upon a more restricted range of approaches, primarily separated from the ongoing activities of the English classroom.[1]

Approaches to Test Preparation

In recent years there has been a widespread call for systemic reform of schools and school systems (e.g., Smith & O'Day, 1991). One part of systemic reform requires alignment between curriculum and assessment. In times such as these, with a widespread focus on achievement scores, how this is done becomes a critical issue. On the one hand, some educators focus primarily on practicing sample test items and helping students become "test wise"; they teach such test-taking skills as ways to select a best answer or how to best respond to a writing task from a reading item. Others advocate teaching the needed literacy abilities throughout the year as part of the regular grade-level curriculum. Even though both groups share good test results as a goal, the first group focuses primarily on improvement in test scores, while the second focuses on raising both test scores and student learning by improving the curriculum.

In our study, we found that while some test practice and test-taking hints were offered in both the effective and typical schools, reformulation of both curriculum *and* instructional practice was a pervasive feature only in the effective schools. Qualitative differences appeared in the ways in which test preparation was conceived and enacted in the effective versus the typical schools:

> **Finding 2**
>
> In effective schools, test preparation does not mean mere practice of test-related items. Rather, the focus is on the underlying knowledge and skills needed to do well in coursework and in life, as well as on the tests, and these become part of the ongoing English language arts learning goals and the students' ongoing received curriculum. In contrast, in the typical schools, test prep means test practice. It is allocated its own space in class time, often before testing begins, apart from the rest of the year's work and goals.

Almost all the teachers we studied used both integrated and separated approaches to test preparation some of the time. However, the dominant patterns of use varied considerably. More than 80 percent of the effective teachers in our study in both kinds of schools integrated the skills and knowledge that were to be tested into the ongoing curriculum as their dominant approach to test preparation; the other effective teachers used integrated and separated approaches about equally. In comparison, 75 percent of the typical teachers used a separated approach to test preparation, primarily teaching test preparation skills and knowledge apart from the ongoing curriculum. Seventeen percent of the typical teachers did not teach test preparation at all, because their students were not scheduled to take a high-stakes test that year (see Appendix C, Table 2).

In the effective schools, both teachers and administrators worked together to deconstruct and analyze sample test items. They often also took the tests themselves. These activities helped them better understand the skills, strategies, and knowledge their students needed in order to do well. Then they reviewed and revised both the curriculum and the instructional guidelines to ensure that the identified skills and knowledge were incorporated into the day-to-day English program of students. Before a test, the format was generally practiced to ensure students' familiarity with it. However, not much teaching time was devoted to this. Rather, it was the infusion of the needed skills and knowledge into the curriculum that seemed to make a difference. Students were also taught to become more reflective about their own reading and writing performance, in some cases using rubrics throughout the school year in order to help them gain insight into their own performance and needs.

Kate McFadden-Midby and Myra LeBendig at Foshay, an effective school, always strove to understand the test demands of the Stanford 9. They helped their students make connections between their ongoing curriculum and academic and real-life situations, including testing. For example, McFadden-Midby collaborated with a group of teachers to design a series of lessons that would incorporate the skills tested by the Stanford 9 into their literature curriculum. They identified certain areas in which their students did least well (e.g., vocabulary, spelling, and reading comprehension) and planned lessons that would integrate their use in meaningful ways into the students' everyday experiences. They developed a series of eight lessons as models to be used with a variety of literature. These lessons served as ways for the teachers to create opportunities to address areas of concern within the regular curriculum.

In effective schools, district-level coordinators often created working groups, and coordinators and teachers collaboratively studied the demands of required high-stakes tests and used their test analyses to rethink the curriculum. For example, when the Florida Writes! Exam was instituted, the Miami-Dade County English language arts central office staff and some teachers met to study and understand the exam and the kinds of demands it made on students. Together, they developed an instructional strategy (grade by grade) that would create yearlong experiences in the different types of writing, including the kinds of organization, elaboration, and polishing that were required. This coordination began some years before our study, and the instructional changes that led to greater coherence were evident in the classrooms we studied. All classes were replete with rich and demanding writing experiences, including direct instruction and help at all stages. In many classes, teachers spent the first five or ten minutes of each period on an exercise assigned on the board for the students to begin alone or with others as they entered. Sometimes this exercise involved completing or writing analogies. Sometimes, after studying how the Florida Writes! Exam questions were constructed, students were asked to develop questions that were structurally similar. They were also given room to play with language by making up other kinds of questions and answers. These activities broadened their repertoire of test-like questions and gave them a fuller knowledge of how test language works. The student work was always discussed in class and connected to how it might be useful not only on a test, but also for their own writing or reading. Connections were made to this activity later in the day, week, or year, as well as across years. For example, Turner Tech's Chris Kirchner said, "Last year my students did a lot with topic sentence and details, so this year I expect to see it in all the writing they do and I can work on other things on the Florida Writes! Exam."

Although the writing scores in some of the Miami-Dade County schools we were studying had gone up, the integrated attention to testing remained. During our two-year study, the focus in Miami-Dade County shifted to improving reading scores, but attention to writing focus remained. After studying the various kinds of reading tasks demanded by their high-stakes tests and comparing it with their existing curriculum, the English language arts staff and teachers developed a new Comprehensive Reading Curriculum Guide. Once again, they developed a series of lessons to permeate the year's curriculum at each grade level.

In some schools, teachers selectively used materials and created activities because they knew that their students needed to practice skills and knowledge that would be tapped by the test but were also needed for higher literacy. For example, Suzanna Matton, an effective teacher at Springfield High, was constantly attuned to enriching her students' vocabulary. She selected words she thought they would need to know, gave them practice, and followed with quizzes every six weeks. She also had her students do a great deal of analytic writing throughout the year, helping them become aware of strategic ways to write a well-developed analytic paper in response to the material they read as well as in response to writing prompts. For example, she helped her students trace how a conflict developed and was worked through in a story, and how allusion was used and to what effect, and then had them write about it, providing evidence. The students also learned to judge their own and others' writing and gained ability in a variety of writing modes.

In contrast, at the typical schools, the primary mode of test preparation offered practice on old editions of the test, teacher-made tests and practice materials, and, sometimes, commercial materials using formats and questions similar to those of the test at hand. In such cases, if test preparation occurred at all, there was a test-taking practice one or two months (or often more) before the exam, or the preparation spanned the entire year but was sporadic and unconnected to other class experiences. Although the Palm Middle School Improvement Plan called for fifteen test-taking practice assignments to be given to the students across the curriculum during the course of the year, these assignments, if done at all, were most often inserted into the curriculum as additions rather than integrated. The focus was on how to take a test, rather than how to gain and use the skills and knowledge tested.

At Dove Middle School, all students in the school, grades 6 through 8, were required to take California's statewide exam. Evangeline Turner, an excellent teacher whose students consistently scored better than those in other classes, was asked by the principal to give a booster course to seventh-grade students who, with help, could most likely raise the scores of the school as a whole. Although the course was short in duration, she focused on helping the students think strategically about how to take the exam and how to distinguish what she calls "on the surface and under the surface" questions. She also had them read books that were highly interesting, culturally relevant, and challenging to discuss, such as *The House on Mango Street*, exploring their understandings and writing about it in test-like ways. Although these were cram sessions, Turner tried to provide the students with ways to read, understand, and write in order to develop abilities that are marks of high literacy, not merely test-passing skills. Throughout the year, in her regular classes, Turner focused on the skills and competencies that are needed to do well on tests and to do well in English. In comparison, most of the other teachers at Dove focused on test prep one week before the test, using a test package provided by the principal.

In other typical schools, some teachers seemed to blame the students, or the test, but not themselves. Although the principal at Hayes is a highly motivating personality and told the faculty, "We can do it,"

there was an underlying belief among the faculty with whom we interacted that the students were not capable of scoring well on the exam.
Teachers did not believe they could make a difference. For example,
Ron Soja said, "They don't know anything. It's like they never did anything." Soja did not seem to feel personally accountable for ensuring
that his students possessed the underlying knowledge and skills to do
well. He said:

> The Stanford test is not a good test to see whether they are
> achieving in school or not, because up until this year it hasn't
> meant anything. Half the kids, they think it's a big joke.

Beginning two years hence, students in this district would need
to achieve a certain percentile score (not yet determined) on the Stanford 9 to be eligible for high school graduation. Soja rationalized that
the students scored badly on the test because they did not take it seriously (did not understand its implications), rather than focusing on his
efforts to prepare them for it. Because the school was on the critically
low list, the principal wanted desperately for the scores to improve
(with threat of receivership if they did not). Although she had a good
relationship with the teachers (she is an ex-English teacher), she had
neither championed nor orchestrated a coherent plan to improve the
teachers' understanding of the test demands and align them with students' needs. Instead, more materials were purchased and some commercial staff development presentations (e.g., about writing across the
curriculum) were purchased. But these were isolated attempts; an
overall plan was not apparent. No teachers ever mentioned the staff
development to us, and we found the English department chair return-
ing new materials because no one wanted to use them. The principal
had tried to institute sustained silent reading during homeroom but
had not yet been able to convince the teachers to accept the fifteen-
minute lengthening of the home room period that this change would
require, nor did they mutually negotiate an alternative time. At Hayes,
the teachers had not been involved in identifying their students' needs
(or their own), nor had a professional discussion been started about the
overall changes needed.

Like Soja, Carol McGuinness did not take personal responsibility
for improving the test scores of her students, nor was she sure of the
relationship between her teaching and their test scores. She said:

> I don't know if what I am doing in my classroom is making
> them better able to handle these tests, but I'm hoping it will
> make them better equipped to handle the really hard choices
> they come up against in life.

In McGuinness's district, the alignment between student needs, curriculum, and assessment was being addressed, but neither she nor her department chair were able to translate the district goals into classroom practice. Even though their school was one of the least effective in the district, the language arts chair said of his department, "We don't meet unless we have to meet. This is not my administrative style. I just put things in their mailboxes."

Practice activities are often developed by states and districts or commercial material developers, but these are not meant to be the sole activity that schools use to help students do well. To prepare for the New York State Regents exam in English, which all students must pass to graduate, one typical New York school sent two teachers to a state education department meeting designed to brief them on grading procedures. They, in turn, transmitted what they had learned to their colleagues. The English language arts district supervisor bought sets of guide booklets for Regents practice, and Elaine Dinardi bought yet another for additional practice. The books present Regents exam–like activities for the students to practice. The department faculty also made up grade-level-specific, take-home finals that followed the Regents format. Dinardi interspersed these practice activities with her usual curriculum until sometime in April, when she began to stress Regents practice in her class. This practice became the major class activity, in effect became the curriculum, for the entire quarter, in preparation for the June exam. Over this time, practice focused on the kinds of essays the test would require: writing for information, comparison and contrast, and critical lens (relating a quote to a work that was read), all presented in the form required by the test. It should be noted that this was the first year that the English Regents exam was mandated for all students. In prior years, the school's percentage of students passing was at or below 50 percent. Consequently, district educators were very apprehensive about the Regents. As at Hayes, teachers at this school did not believe the average student had the capability to perform well on the test.

Administrators of typical schools sometimes purchased professional services or programs that were not integrated into the ongoing program. For example, at Hendricks an outside consultant was hired to give test-taking strategy workshops to tenth-grade students to help improve their scores. The prepackaged materials exhibited little understanding of the specific test or the needs of the students.

While most of the typical schools in our study had developed school improvement plans, these had been conceived and put into place as separate, rather than conceptually coherent, experiences for students, offering such additions as pullout programs, tutorials, packaged computer-assisted programs, and other predesigned instructional programs that did not necessarily connect to overarching curricular goals and ongoing classroom experiences. Nor had there been an effort to selectively use these instructional additions to support greater conceptual coherence across students' English language arts experiences.

Overall, effective schools seemed to focus on students' learning, using the tests to be certain that the skills and knowledge tested were being learned within the framework of improved language arts instruction, while the typical schools seemed to focus on the tests themselves, with raising test scores, rather than students' literacy learning, as the primary goal.

Connecting Learnings

The education literature on learning and instruction is replete with evidence that students' learning and recall are more likely to be enhanced when they can connect new learnings to what they already know—from both in- and out-of-school experiences—than when the content of instruction is treated as if it is entirely new (see for example, Bransford, Brown, & Cocking, 1999; Brown & Campione, 1996). Well-developed knowledge is also linked with important concepts, and its relevance to other concepts is well understood. Although many curriculum guides, as well as scope and sequence charts, have attempted to make links between specific learnings within and across the grades, the connections have too often been implicit at best, and they often remain in the mind of the teacher or curriculum developer rather than being shared with the students (see Applebee, 1996).

Findings from our study indicate that connectedness is a pervasive goal of the teachers and administrators in the effective schools:

> **Finding 3**
>
> In effective schools, overt connections are constantly made between knowledge, skills, and ideas across lessons, classes, and grades as well as across in-school and out-of-school applications. In contrast, in the typical schools, connections are more often unspoken or implicit, if they are made at all. More often, the lessons, units, and curricula are treated as disconnected entities.

At least 88 percent of the effective teachers in our study in both types of schools tended to make all three kinds of connections—within lessons, across lessons, and across in-school and out-of-school applications—with approximately equal focus. In comparison, the typical teachers tended to make no connections at all, and those that were made tended to be "real-world" connections between school and home, without connection back to the text or the topic at hand. None of the typical teachers emphasized all three types of connections (see Appendix C, Table 3).

In the effective schools, the effective teachers worked consciously to weave a web of connections. At Springfield High School, Celeste Rotondi planned her lessons with consideration of the ways in which they connected with each other, with test demands, and with the students' growing knowledge. For example, when discussing her goals for the reading of *Invisible Man* by Ralph Ellison, she said:

> My primary goal is to provide them with what I consider a challenging piece of literature that will give them an excellent resource for the AP exam. It fits in well with the works we have studied in that it explores the inner consciousness and makes use of a recurring image/symbol that has been the key to several other literary works . . . that of blindness. It allows them to explore the way a symbol can convey meaning in several literary works. Personally, I feel that Ellison's is a monumental literary work. The ramifications in terms of social psychology with the concept of invisibility applies to so many different life experiences. I try to open the students' appreciation of how this work relates to their own world, and it introduces them to the question of identity and how the daily interactions are crucial to identity formation.

Thus, her lessons connected texts, tests, and life.

Tawanda Richardson, an effective teacher at the effective Drew Middle School, was a literacy coach. Coaches were hired by the district to work with teachers, to suggest, demonstrate, and share ideas for improved instruction; the coaching program developed a mentoring relationship matching highly successful teachers with new ones in ways that could effect professional growth and improve student performance. It invited teachers into a systemwide support network. Although Richardson was familiar with the districtwide curriculum, she felt she also needed to understand the particular teacher and class with whom she would work. To do this, she observed, gathered data about the class, and tried to understand student and teacher needs. She then set up goals with the teacher and demonstrated lessons—goals and strategies that met the students' needs but were intrinsically connected to the larger curriculum.

Springfield High School, an effective school that was preparing for accreditation, was in the process of revising its mission and approaches to education. Self-study led the teachers to develop a more integrated approach to learning, fostering connections both within school and between school and community. One part of the mission statement focused on students as effective communicators. Faculty were collaboratively working in teams to ensure that the skills needed for effective communication would be taught and reinforced across the grades and across the curriculum. This process was followed for the other components of the school's mission as well, and these were coordinated with the California state standards. And teachers were aware of these connections. For example, Celeste Rotondi said:

> Standards, as much as they're a kind of pain in the butt when we have these meetings and align the standards and all that stuff, it has helped me. . . . My curriculum is strong. But once I started really looking at the standards I realized I didn't have a lot of oral writing activities [that is, speaking activities, where students compose orally], and so it kind of helped me to conceptualize that a little better and forced me to incorporate that.

It never occurred to Rotondi to simply add a few oral activities to her lesson plans. Instead, she rethought how reading, writing, and oral language could be interrelated across the curriculum and across the year in ways that would strengthen her students' oral as well as written communication abilities.

In addition to establishing connectedness of goals, skills, and experiences across the day and year (connections Rotondi would plan and make overt to her students when appropriate), she also wanted to ensure that her students could learn to make connections across the literature they were reading, as well as connections from literature to life. She wanted her students to learn to read the text and the world. To do this, Rotondi organized her literature instruction around thematic units, for example pairing *The Glass Menagerie* and *A Raisin in the Sun* to permit her students to focus on family relationships and ways in which families deal with the situations they face. For such units, she typically created study guides that provided scaffolding for her students and made overt to both her students and herself the particular connections that were in focus. Comparisons across the pieces helped her students compare and critique aspects of structure, language, and style while they also focused on thematic elements across the pieces and connected (e.g., compared and critiqued) them based on related situations in the world today.

In contrast, in the typical schools, even when the lessons were integrated within a unit, there was little interweaving across lessons; few overt connections were made among the content, knowledge (literary or otherwise), and skills being taught. Class lessons were often treated as separate wholes—with a particular focus introduced, practiced, discussed, and then put aside. For example, Ron Soja (Hayes High School) said that in his yearlong plans, he moved the students from more subjective to more objective writing tasks. However, we saw no indication that he shared this distinction with his students or helped them make other connections among the kinds of writing he assigned.

Monica Matthews often had her middle school students write about the literature they had read. However, the connections among the students' own writing and the works they had read were not explicitly made, nor did she help her students make connections between the literature they read and the larger world.

At Stockton Middle School, Helen Ross asked questions that encouraged her students to make connections, but because discussions were carefully controlled, the connections the students would make were predetermined. For example, when they read *The Diary of Anne Frank* in play form, taking turns reading parts, she asked, "These are real people your age. How would you react in that situation?" "What would you do?" Although these questions seem open-ended, she was actually leading in a particular direction, toward the diary. She steered the discussion with questions and comments until a student came forth with the idea she sought. Then she said, "Her diary. That's how she escapes," marking the conclusion of that day's discussion.

This same pattern of questioning can also be seen in Carol McGuinness's high school class; in this example, she opened the discussion after reading a chapter of Jamake Highwater's *Anpao: An American Indian Odyssey.*

Teacher:	In the Judeo-Christian tradition, do we have animals that converse with God?
Student 1:	No.
Teacher:	Only one, and which one is that?
Student 2:	The snake.
Teacher:	The snake. Representative of _____?
Students:	Satan.
Teacher:	Right. Satan. In this case the animals are benevolent. They are not evil. How is humanity according to this legend?

Rather than encouraging her students to make their own connections, or showing them how, McGuinness guided them to guess the connection she had made. Following this very short pseudo-discussion,

McGuinness had the students sequence twenty-four events that she had taken from the first chapters of the text. This sequencing activity was disconnected from the discussion that had preceded it and was to be followed by another disconnected activity the next day, when she planned to have them act out a scene from the text.

The lack of connectedness in the classrooms of Ross and McGuinness was also reflected in the larger curriculum across the grades; their departments did not foster connectedness. For example, in Ross's district, department chairs in the middle and high schools were eliminated a few years ago in favor of a K–12 English language arts coordinator for the district's schools. He had been trying to foster curriculum coherence and continuity through cross-grade dialogue and within-grade curriculum coordination; however, because of his many responsibilities, he had difficulty accomplishing all of his goals. As he told us, "Too many buildings, too many kids, too many teachers. I just can't do what I want anywhere. So I do what I can. You have to keep your sights limited to what you can do." He had begun to make a difference, with some teachers working to create connections in their curriculum and instruction, but he had not yet managed to transform the approaches of whole departments.

Although the central office in McGuinness's district was making monumental efforts to make the language arts program more cohesive, her department chair at Hendricks made little effort to follow through with his teachers. He said that although he gets good ideas and materials from the central office, he just puts the packages in the teachers' mailboxes instead of meeting, discussing, planning, and collaboratively developing ways to incorporate the ideas into the curriculum.

A lack of connection was also found in the other typical schools. For example, in selecting materials and planning lessons, there was often no overall plan connecting the parts. And when workshops and materials had been selected, their relationship to the whole program was overlooked. For example, Palm Middle School hired a private company to provide workshops designed to help teachers do student-centered learning. However, there was no attempt to integrate the company's predesigned program with the new English language arts curriculum, or with any other ongoing aspect of the school's program.

In the typical schools, when educators gained information from professional encounters or adopted predeveloped programs or commercial materials, they seemed not to use them in the full and integrated ways in which they were intended. Connie McGee, an English language arts supervisor for the Miami-Dade County Schools, calls it the "Key Lime Pie syndrome": even though a set of activities has been planned, demonstrated, and explained within a particular rationale and sequence, with features that build on each other, some teachers choose only the parts that appeal to them. McGee says, "I show them how to make the whole pie, but they make just the meringue or just the filling and wonder why it doesn't taste like key lime pie." The resulting failure of the activities is then blamed on the poor "recipe" or the poor students rather than lack of a coordinated whole.[2]

Enabling Strategies

During the past twenty-five or more years, a sizable research literature has emphasized the contribution of students' strategic awareness to learning and performance, as well as the importance of teaching students strategies for carrying out reading, writing, and thinking tasks (e.g., Hillocks, 1995; Paris, Wasik, & Turner, 1991; Pressley et al., 1994). It is important for students to learn not only content, but also intentional ways of thinking and doing. In response, instructional approaches have been developed to help students become aware not only of the content but also of particular tasks. While the fields of science and mathematics have always seemed to be natural environments for teaching strategic approaches that enhance student performance (e.g.,. the scientific method, steps to mathematical solutions), teaching strategies and helping students to be strategic in the ways in which they approach a task (e.g., process approaches to writing, reflective literacy, or reciprocal teaching) are newer to the English language arts.

In our study, we found explicit differences in how teachers teach students strategies that will enable them to successfully engage in activities on their own and to reflect on and monitor their own learning:

> **Finding 4**
>
> In effective schools, students in English language arts classes are overtly taught strategies for thinking as well as doing. In contrast, in typical schools, the focus is on the content or skill, without overtly teaching the overarching strategies for planning, organizing, completing, or reflecting on the content or activity.

All of the effective teachers in our study overtly taught their students strategies for organizing their thoughts and completing tasks, while only 17 percent of the typical teachers did so. The other 83 percent of the typical teachers left such strategies implicit (see Appendix C, Table 4).

In the effective schools, the teachers segmented new or difficult tasks, providing their students with guides for ways to accomplish them. However, the help they offered was not merely procedural; rather, it was designed so that the students would understand how to do well. Sometimes the teachers provided models and lists, sometimes evaluation rubrics. Strategies for how to do the task, as well as how to think about the task, were discussed and modeled, and reminder sheets were developed for student use. These strategies provided the students with ways to work through the tasks themselves, helping them to understand and meet the task's demands. For instance, Cathy Starr taught her students strategies to use to reflect on their progress as they moved through an activity.[3] After a research activity, the students were to rate themselves on their research and writing using rubrics they had developed:

1. Where do you think you fall for the research [grade yourself]? Did you spend the time trying to find the information? Did you keep going until you had learned enough to write your report?

2. Whether this is a short and informal or a longer and more formal piece, you should spend time thinking about the writing. Did you plan what you were going to say? Did you think about it? Did you review it and revise it before putting it in the back [of the classroom]?

3. Did you edit? Did you check the spelling and punctuation?

Most of the teachers in the effective schools shared and discussed with students rubrics for evaluating performance; they also incorporated them into their ongoing instructional activities as a way to help their students develop an understanding of the components that contribute to a higher score (more complete, more elaborated, more highly organized response). Use of the rubrics also helped students develop reflection and repair strategies relevant to their reading, writing, and oral presentation activities.

Alicia Alliston, an effective teacher at Drew Middle School, provided her students with strategies for making entries in their Reader's Journal. First, they learned that the Journal had several parts: the heading with the title and author, an entry number, an illustration relevant to that week's section of reading, a quick summary, an overall response/reaction to the reading, a writing aid if needed (e.g., "The most _____ part of the reading was _____ because . . ." or "The part of the story or character that caught my attention was _____ because . . ."), and other possible sections (e.g., triggered memory, prediction, advice, evaluation). Written responses were required to be a minimum of two pages long, and when the task was new, Alliston provided the students with a preformatted form to use as a guide. She also provided them with suggestions and tips about what to include in their response, such as what a reaction should include, how to highlight an interesting passage and selectively discuss its features, and questions to consider. She also offered starters for them to use when stumped (e.g., "I wonder . . . ," "I noticed . . . ," "I felt . . ."). When they did creative writing, she gave students sheets suggesting formats and purposes, such as providing advice, diary entry, or poetry. She also supplied starters or models and gave students suggestions for the kinds of illustrations they might choose, such as a hand-drawn picture, a cutout from a magazine or newspaper, or a computer graphic.

Kate McFadden-Midby at Foshay also provided her students with strategies for completing a task well if she thought it was going to be new or challenging. For example, when her students were learning to do character analyses and to understand differing perspectives, she asked them to begin by developing a critical thinking question and then to choose two characters from the book (or books) they had read, in order to compare the characters' viewpoints on that question. The critical thinking questions needed to be ones that anyone could discuss even without having read the book (e.g., one student asked, "Why are people so cruel when it comes to revenge?"). Before students met in groups, McFadden-Midby provided this outline:

> (1) share your critical thinking question with your group; (2) tell your group partners why you chose that particular question and what situation in the book made you think about it; and, (3) tell which two characters you have chosen to discuss that question in a miniplay.

The students engaged in deep and substantive discussion about their classmates' questions, because McFadden-Midby's strategy list had helped them gain clarity about the goals and process of the task. The next day, these discussions were followed by a prewriting activity in preparation for writing a description of the characters they chose. McFadden-Midby instructed students on how to develop a T-chart on which one character's name is placed at the top of one column of the T and the other character at the top of the other column. She told them to list characteristics: what their characters were like, experiences they had, opinions, and so on. She provided them with strategies to identify characteristics and then compare them across the two characters.

This was followed by group sharing, where the students presented their characters. Here, McFadden-Midby scaffolded her students' thinking by asking questions about the characters: "What kind of person was the mother? What are some adjectives that might describe her? How do you think those things could influence how she feels?" Over time, when the students had been helped to develop deeper understandings of their characters through a variety of supportive strategies, they were then helped to write a miniplay depicting those same characters involved in the issue they had raised in their critical thinking question. Although this was a highly complex activity, the students were provided with supportive strategies along the way, gaining insight not merely into the characters themselves, but also into ways they could understand characters and differing perspectives when reading and writing on their own.

In the typical schools, instruction focused on the content or the skill, but not necessarily on providing students with procedural or metacognitive strategies. For example, in Carol McGuinness's tenth-grade class, two of the three groups of students involved in the sequencing activity mentioned earlier were having some difficulty putting the twenty-four events in sequence. Rather than eliciting any strategies that might be useful, McGuinness simply told them,

> OK. Divide your slips into thirds. OK? This is research. Start with the beginning, the middle, and the end and put the strips into three different piles. Get this done and you'll have a method.

But her guidance did not help the students understand the concept of sequencing any better, nor what it meant to create temporal order from story. Only one group of students seemed to understand what she meant and completed the task. So although McGuinness wanted her students to practice the skill of sequencing, she provided them with little guidance for doing so, either with her help or on their own.

The English chair at one of the typical schools, speaking about his teachers in general, said, "Incorporating strategies is difficult for most of us because it's hard for us to pull ourselves out of our comfort range. You know, unless we're prepared to teach the strategy, we're inclined to do something the old way." In contrast, Evangeline Turner, an effective teacher in another typical school (Drew Middle School), always taught her students strategies and reminded them to use them throughout the year. For example, she gave her students rubrics for how to make and judge an oral presentation, and how to think, reach interpretations, and then justify their responses. She helped them learn to think metacognitively and to explain their ideas. Jonathan Luther, a newer teacher, had been teaching to the test throughout the year, with a primary focus on form (e.g., grammar, vocabulary, structure); however, he had come to realize that empowering his students with strategies would contribute more toward improving both their literacy development and their test scores. He began working with Turner to do this. Strategy instruction has yet to be picked up by other teachers, although Turner is the department chair and is trying to help them do so.

Conceptions of Learning

"What counts as knowing" has become a much-used phrase in the educational literature. It is often used to make distinctions between educators who focus on facts and concepts and those who focus on students' abilities to think about and use new knowledge. At one time, a student's ability to give definitions, select right answers, and fill deleted information into sentences and charts was considered evidence of learning. But at least two bodies of research changed that: one focused on disciplinary initiation, where the goal became to help students learn to approximate more and more closely expert thinking in particular fields, such as thinking like a historian (e.g., Bazerman, 1981); the other focused on critical thinking, particularly on higher levels of cognitive manipulation of the material (e.g., Langer & Applebee, 1987; Schallert, 1976). More recently, the issue has turned to engagement (Guthrie & Alvermann, 1999). Here, concern goes beyond time on task to student involvement with the material. Although all three bodies of work have had an effect on literacy pedagogy, a recent National Assessment of Educational Progress report (1998) indicates that fewer than 7 percent of students in grades 4, 8, and 12 perform at the "advanced" level, the highest of four possible achievement levels in reading. This level represents students' grade-appropriate ability to deal analytically with challenging subject matter and to apply this knowledge to real-world situations.

Findings from our study suggest distinct differences in teachers' conceptions of learning in the effective versus the typical schools:

> **Finding 5**
>
> In effective schools, the tenor of the instructional environment is such that, even after students reach achievement goals, English language arts teachers move students beyond them toward

deeper understandings of and ability to generate ideas and knowledge. In contrast, in the typical schools, once students exhibit use of the immediate understandings or skills in focus, teachers move on to another lesson.

All of the effective teachers in our study took a generative approach to student learning, going beyond students' acquisition of the skills or knowledge to engaging them in deeper understandings. In comparison, all of the typical teachers moved on to other goals and activities once they had evidence that the targeted skills or knowledge had been learned (see Appendix C, Table 5).

For example, in Myra LeBendig's class at Foshay, both students and teacher expected their lessons to be highly thought-provoking and generative. When studying *Invisible Man* by Ralph Ellison, LeBendig often asked her students to think about the character's situation and the various attitudes and ethics it portrayed. After the more obvious themes in the text were discussed, LeBendig and the students worked together to explore the text from many points of view, both from within the text and from life. But they didn't stop there. LeBendig then helped her students discuss ideas and issues generated by the text that involved their own ethnicity. As part of the cultural knowledge generated during these lessons, the discussion was interlaced with references by both teacher and students to famous people (e.g., Malcolm X, W. E. B. Du Bois) and to other works that students might be interested in reading. In LeBendig's class, ideas begat ideas and discussion and led to deeper understandings of the text as well as life.

Alicia Alliston at Drew Middle School never stopped her literature lessons when she was confident her students had understood the book and developed their own defensible interpretations. Once they arrived at this level of expertise, she provided an array of activities that provoked her students to think and learn more. For example, when her students were reading and writing about *The Midwife's Apprentice* by Karen Cushman, they also discussed the history, life, and art of the Renaissance. They did research into the life and social patterns of the period and ended with a Renaissance Faire.

Celeste Rotondi (Springfield High School) had her students work in literature circles in which they discussed both the commonalities and the differences in the books they read. Literature circle time was her students' opportunity to go beyond the texts they were reading, as more mature discussants and critics. One literature circle involved students in reading the following teacher-selected books: *The Great Gatsby; Bless Me, Ultima; Slaughterhouse Five;* and *Always Running:*

La Vida Loca, Gang Days in L.A. At the end of the cycle of discussions, the students wrote and performed songs about the books and their deeper meanings and created CD cases with fictional song titles, covers, and artists.

Alliston's class also read *Night* by Elie Wiesel. To prepare for it, Alliston had her students look at photos from concentration camps and write down words and phrases that were relevant. These were used to create poems. While reading *Night*, the class visited the Museum of Tolerance, completed an assignment while they were there, and wrote letters from three points of view (seven to choose from), all involved in some way with the Holocaust. Thus the reading of *Night* offered not only a chance to develop an understanding and critique of the work itself (though this was done), but rather an integrated opportunity to contemplate historical, ethical, political, and personal issues raised by the reading.

In contrast, in the typical schools, the learning activity and the thinking about it seemed to stop with the responses sought or the assigned task completed—at a level Vygotsky (1978) calls "pseudo concepts," in which the learning is more a superficial recalling of names, definitions, and facts than a deeper and more highly conceptualized learning.

For example, when Jack Foley's class at New Westford High read *To Kill a Mockingbird*, he asked questions about the content and vocabulary. He called on students to provide the answers and, when they did, he either added additional comments to their responses or moved on to the next question. Neither the text nor the students' responses were used during the discussion to generate historical, social, or other connections and elaborations.

After reading *Romeo and Juliet*, Ron Soja gave his students the following issues and asked them to select the one they most "leaned" toward: Romeo and Juliet are victims of fate, Romeo and Juliet are victims of society, or Romeo and Juliet are victims of their own passions. The next day they discussed their selections and reasons, then Soja went on to the next topic.

At Hendricks High School, Carol McGuinness ended her lessons when her students provided the answer she was after. Using the example of the sequencing activity again, as soon as the first group finished, McGuinness asked them to read the strips in sequence. Then the activity was over, even though the other groups were in the midst of struggling with the task. No connection was made either to the chapter as a whole or to the forthcoming chapter, nor to sequencing itself as a sometimes useful skill. Even the fact that the teacher was willing to end the task before all but one group had finished was evidence of the lack of value that was attributed to it as a thought-provoking learning experience. Similarly, when her students studied verb tenses, they were given a homework sheet that was a continuation of what they were doing in class. It was more of the same, rather than a generative activity that builds upon the new knowledge.

Thus, in the effective schools students were constantly encouraged to go beyond the basic learning experiences in challenging and enriching ways. In contrast, students in the typical schools had few opportunities for more creative and critical experiences.

Classroom Organization

In recent years, a variety of approaches to classroom organization have been proposed to provide students with more opportunities to learn through substantive interaction with one another as well as with the teacher. These approaches include collaborative (Barnes, 1976) and cooperative groups (Slavin, et al., 1996), literature clubs (Raphael & McMahon, 1994), peer writing groups (Graves, 1983), and envisionment-building classrooms (Langer, 1995). These and other similar approaches have been developed in response to both theory and research from a sociocognitive orientation that sees interactive working groups focused on shared problems as providing supportive environments for learning. Bakhtin's (1981) notion of heteroglossia (see also Nystrand, 1997) suggests that all learning is dialogic, reliant on and gaining meaning from the many past and present relevant voices. In dialogic groups, students bring their personal, cultural, and academic knowledge to the interaction as they play the multiple roles of learners, teachers, and inquirers, and in so doing they have an opportunity to consider the issue at hand from multiple perspectives. Students can interact as both problem generators and problem solvers. New ideas can be entertained and new ways of thinking modeled as more and less expert knowers of the content and those more and less familiar with the task share expertise, provide feedback, and learn from each other. Such contexts emphasize shared cognition, in which the varied contributions of the participants allow the group to achieve more than individuals could on their own. However, several studies have indicated that such groupings are not pervasive in American schools (NAEP, 1998; Applebee, 1993; Nystrand, Gamoran, & Heck, 1993). Findings from our Excellence in English study suggest that even when students meet in groups, there are qualitative differences between how the groups are used by teachers and enacted by students:

Finding 6

In effective schools, English learning and high literacy (the content as well as the skills) are treated as social activity, with depth and complexity of understanding and proficiency with conventions growing from students' interaction with present and imagined others. In contrast, in typical schools, students tend to work alone or interact with the teacher, and when collaborative or group work occurs, the activity focuses on answering questions rather than engaging in substantive discussion from multiple perspectives.

In the effective schools, at least 96 percent of the teachers we studied helped students engage in the thoughtful dialogue we call shared cognition. These teachers expected their students not merely to work together, but to sharpen their understandings with, against, and from each other. In comparison, teachers in the typical schools focused on individual thinking. Even when their students worked together, the thinking was parallel as opposed to dialogic (see Appendix C, Table 6).

In the effective schools, students not only worked together in physical proximity, but they also gained skill in sharing ideas, reacting to each other, testing out ideas and arguments, and contributing to the intellectual tenor of the class. They engaged in the kind of teamwork that is now so highly prized in business and industry, though sometimes suspect in school settings, where solitary work is still too often prized.

All the classes at International High School work collaboratively. In Marsha Slater's class, from the first days of school and throughout the year, students were taught to work together, discussing issues and reacting to each others' ideas even as they were gaining a common language through which to communicate. (All students at International are recent immigrants.) During one of the first few weeks of school, Slater introduced a literature research and writing activity that required group work throughout. The students divided into groups and started planning their strategy. We saw a similar pattern in science, where the students were graphing and mapping on computer the results of their group-accomplished experiments. It is part of the educational philosophy of the school that "the most successful educational programs are those that emphasize high expectations coupled with effective support systems; individuals learn best from each other in collaborative groupings." Throughout our study, Slater's emphasis was on collaborative and active learning. Activity guides helped the students in a group work together toward a common goal, but debriefing sessions and conferences provided a time for each student to discuss not only the group's work but also her or his own areas of accomplishment and need.[4] In all the effective schools, such collaborative activities were common. Students worked together to develop the best thinking or best paper (or other product) they collectively could; they helped and learned within the same activity as in life.

In the effective schools, even whole-class activities, particularly discussion, were used to foster similar cognitive collaborations. At Foshay, although her students sometimes worked in groups, Myra LeBendig often favored whole-class discussions. She used discussion as a time for exchanging ideas and stimulating thought, exploration, and explanation. As a whole class, her students were taught to work together, listening to and interacting with one another about the ideas at hand. For example, throughout one whole-class discussion about *Invisible Man*, her students raised ideas and freely engaged in literary dialogue. One student brought up the issue of how race was treated in the book, and another the symbolism of blindness as ignorance (as portrayed in the book). One student said he thought Dr. Bledsoe "had self-hatred," in response to which a classmate said she thought it wasn't self-hatred but that Bledsoe didn't know where he fit in and didn't know how to connect his two cultural parts: "He hasn't found himself. He's in between." This generated a discussion that continued for half an hour, with the students in deep discussion about their interpretations of the text and its connection to social issues of identity. LeBendig explained that she uses such discussions to help students "work through their evolving understandings, ideas, and opinions that will change as they continue reading the book." She explained that early in the year she told her students, "Fight to teach me," meaning she wanted them to disagree with her (and each other) and extend her (and their) thinking with their comments. This is exactly what they did in class discussion.

At the same school, Kate McFadden-Midby's classes often worked in collaborative groups. Group Share was a common activity, during which students came up with interesting questions about what they were reading for the group to consider and discuss. When it was group time, the students immediately began interacting in productive ways. They knew what to do and were eager to interact. McFadden-Midby explained that early in the school year she told students about her expectations, time management, and ways in which their thinking was valued. Her goal was to have her students truly share ideas and stimulate each other's thinking by engaging in real conversations. We have already seen how she orchestrated such activities, in the example of her lessons on character analysis presented in the section on strategy instruction. In that example, the students worked together to sharpen their individual and collective understandings of characters in books they had read, even though they had read different books. In turn, the understandings that emerged from those discussions helped the students to develop rich characters in miniplays of their own. Throughout, they were absorbed in discussion and thought.

At Hudson Middle School, Cathy Starr used both whole-class and small-group activities. They were woven into one another and together supported students' developing thinking. For example, as a response to assigned reading, she asked her students to bring three thought-provoking questions to class to stimulate discussion. Students met in groups to discuss these questions and come up with one or two "big" questions for the entire class to discuss. Starr moved from group to group, modeling questions and comments, and provoking deeper discussion and analysis. After the whole-class discussion, Starr listed on the board items on which the students had agreed, as well as issues that still needed to be resolved. In both small groups and whole-class discussions, the students needed to interact in thoughtful ways; the social activity was critical to moving their understandings forward and doing well. These discussions were interspersed with assignments the students were to complete in groups. For example, while reading *The Giver*, Starr gave the following assignment:

Group Task 1—Government [This is one of a set of four.]

Form a group of no less than three and no more than five students to complete this task.

Review the chapters we have read. Design a chart that illustrates how the government for this community functions. Include all information you can find about who makes the decisions and who has power in the community. Include the roles of the individuals in this structure.

This task required the students not merely to locate information, but to discuss and refine what they meant by government and how it functions in the story, as well as the implicit roles the various characters serve.[5] We came to call such working groups "mind to mind," stressing the thoughtfulness the teachers expected.

In classes in the typical schools, such collaborative work rarely took place. For example, Monica Matthews at Crestwood Middle School explained that she has tried to have her students work in groups but "they're unruly." She had them work together in groups minimally "because they talk off-task." In the occasional times when her students did group work, Matthews expected them to turn in individual papers. Thus, their cognitive interaction about ideas was minimal, and their focus was on completing tasks on their own.

This same notion was echoed by high school teacher Elba Rosales. She "saved" group work for the honors and AP classes, claiming that the regular students require more lecture and don't handle group work well. Often the group work that was assigned to what she considers her higher-functioning classes required the students to work independently to complete their part of a task, then put the pieces together as a final product. For example, after reading *Animal Farm*, each group was to create an Animal Farm Newspaper. However, each group member selected a segment (e.g., obituary, horoscope, cartoon, editorial) and completed it as homework; then the pieces were assembled into a four-page newspaper. While the group effort could be said to reflect what happens at a real news office, the students missed opportunities to work through ideas together for each of the components that was incorporated into the final product.

In other classes, group work often took place, but the students didn't "chew ideas" together, nor challenge each other intellectually. They cooperated in completing the task but didn't work conceptualizations through as a group. For example, when Jack Foley's high school students worked together doing study guides, they kept the guides in front of them, moving from item to item down the page. As one student called out the answer, the others wrote it onto their worksheets, and together they moved on to the next question.

Thus, there is an essential difference in the way social activity was carried out, with the effective teachers treating students as members of dynamic learning communities that rely on social and cognitive interactions to support learning.[6] In contrast, the typical teachers in typical schools tended to treat each learner separately, with the assumption that interaction would either diminish the thinking or disrupt the discipline. However, since the schools in this study had similar student bodies, it became evident that the students were more actively engaged in their school work more of the time when English and literacy were treated as social activity.

What Have We Learned about Instruction?

In all, our studies of more effective and typical schools point out the following distinguishing features of effective instruction:

1. Skills and knowledge are taught in a variety of ways using separated, simulated, and integrated instruction.

2. Tests are analyzed to understand the underlying skills and knowledge that go beyond test prep to the literacies needed for school and life. These are then integrated into the ongoing curriculum the students experience.

3. Coherence is achieved because connections in content and structure are made overt within and across activities and units throughout the year and across the grades.

4. Strategies for thinking and doing are emphasized to ensure that students learn procedures for approaching, thinking about, completing, and monitoring the literacy tasks at hand.

5. Generative learning is encouraged to help students use new ideas and learnings to go beyond the lesson or activity and to further their critical and creative thinking and conceptual growth.

6. Classrooms are organized to foster collaboration and cogitation, helping students hear and weigh ideas and perspectives, become inquisitive and reflective, and learn with and from each other.

These features dominated the effective English language arts programs, and they come to life in many of the portraits presented later in this book. As the next chapter demonstrates, the programs that are characterized by these features are also characterized by something else: a supportive environment that enriches teachers' professional lives.

3 Teachers' Professional Lives in Effective Schools

While the effective schools differed from each other in many ways, there was one thing in particular they all shared: they provided an environment that fostered teacher professionalism. Some had joined partnerships advocating whole-school change, whereas others focused more on changes in English and literacy. Yet patterns in the teachers' professional lives were similar to each other—and distinctly different from those of their counterparts in the typical schools. As we analyzed patterns across the schools, we saw six common features in the professional lives of the teachers that contributed to student success. The effective schools in our study all nurtured a climate that:

1. coordinates efforts to improve student achievement,
2. fosters teacher participation in a variety of professional activities,
3. creates instructional improvement activities in ways that offer teachers a strong sense of agency,
4. values commitment to the profession of teaching,
5. engenders caring toward students and colleagues, and
6. fosters respect for learning as a normal part of life.

These characteristics pervaded the effective schools and revealed themselves in the ways that both administrators and teachers viewed their roles and did their jobs. Below, I describe these characteristics by giving examples of how they obtained in some of the effective programs we studied and had not yet obtained in the program at one of the typical schools.

Coordinating Efforts to Improve Achievement

Each of the effective English programs was marked by a highly organized, connected, and overt effort to improve student performance. Although organizational hierarchies differed from locality to locality, there was always a coordinated effort by teachers and administrators to identify needs, investigate and then develop strategies for improvement, and set into motion a variety of processes to help teachers gain the knowledge to effectively incorporate the new practices into their daily routines. Schools and districts made resources for professional development available to teachers in a number of ways, including hiring consultants and speakers to discuss the specific issues of concern to the teachers and administrators; sharing pertinent professional materials; and encouraging teachers to attend professional events and identify ideas that seemed promising for addressing the district's or school's concerns. These ideas were shared and debated, leading to targeted local plans for instruction that would be orchestrated across grades and over time.

Thus it was quite clear that the teachers we studied in Miami-Dade County were working on particular targeted reading and writing competencies, and that these foci reverberated across classrooms and grades. Their shared focus was on higher literacy as well as on student achievement on tests. Their coordinated efforts ensured the coherence between policy and instruction that Cohen (1995) calls for. For example, in all classes we studied, the first five to ten minutes of each class day were devoted to activities that focused on key areas of concern, including the structure and uses of English (e.g., grammar, metaphor, affixes). Often there were separated or simulated activities that were referred back to in later classes. Writing activities for a wide range of purposes were interwoven into the ongoing integrated activities of every classroom, and reciprocal teaching as well as critical thinking activities were common. Each of the skills and strategies being taught and practiced had been carefully developed by the teachers and central office staff. Although these skills had been identified in response to statewide achievement content as well as test results, they were incorporated into the students' coherent and ongoing English language arts experiences, contextualized in terms of purpose, and related to uses in other activities. Class performance and teacher-made tests counted a great deal, but whenever the high-stakes test results arrived, both teachers and central staff reviewed them and used them to reflect on their own practices. They checked to see if rethinking or further coordination was needed. They also stayed abreast of issues and ideas in the field and were aware of the latest as well as the tried-and-true teaching approaches that are highly regarded for supporting particular kinds of learning. When deciding upon new instructional foci, they selected experts who were theoretically compatible with their pedagogical views to learn from so that they could start shaping change in ways they believed would be most appropriate for the Miami-Dade County students. Each year, they expected to make some changes—sometimes adjustments, other times more major shifts in curricular goals and instructional approaches.

Even as student performance improved, teachers set higher goals. The Miami-Dade County Comprehensive Reading Plan is a good example. After a multiyear focus on writing with the aim of improving performance on the Florida Writes! Exam (including a plethora of workshops, as well as discussion groups and the development of model "practice books" for teachers that were full of test goals, sample items, teaching models, ideas, frameworks, and hints), and a concomitant rise in class performance as well as in scores on that exam, the district began to see the need for a comparable refocusing on reading. Hence a professional effort was undertaken to learn about recent ideas for improving achievement in reading, followed by careful redevelopment of the curriculum by a partnership of teachers and supervisors, and the eventual hiring of eighteen reading specialists (key teachers from district schools) to help implement the new plan. (Later, this number was almost doubled.) They worked to augment and improve the English curriculum while maintaining consistency with its constructivist and literature-rich orientations. Among the teaching components they decided together to add were a focus on reciprocal teaching, CRISS (Creating Independence Through Student-owned Strategies), and the America Reads tutorial program. After an initiation period, when they were immersed in coordinating the plan and its new instructional components with the ongoing curriculum, with the state and district standards, with benchmarks, and with assessment tools, the reading specialists began to support teachers in incorporating these foci into their classrooms through workshops, model teaching, sharing sessions, and other face-to-face interactions.

Focal literacy experiences, knowledge, and skills reverberated within and across classrooms, desired learnings were made overt, and teachers as well as students received the support they needed in order to succeed. The comprehensive plan included some specifically planned opportunities to learn. Here are some that Norma Bossard, the district's director of language arts/reading, described in an address at a Miami Literary Celebration (March 1998).

> What's in it for the students for whom this plan was designed? . . . In the days of your parents and my parents, when one dropped out of school for whatever reason, it was an economy that could absorb them. They could earn a living by the

sweat of their brow, with their hands, and with the strength of
their backs. Now the muscle one must use is located between
the two ears. So we must educate children from the neck up. . . .
And so we have written a plan we hope will take into account
all of the opportunities to learn to read that our students
deserve. . . . The opportunity to have the time it takes to learn to
read well. . . .

Included in her plan are the following: two hours of reading
instruction daily, thirty minutes of free reading at school, and a recommended thirty minutes of free reading at home; opportunity across
subjects including a content-area focus on (and professional support
for) reading, including feedback through benchmarks and assessment;
and an opportunity for extended professional development.

The plan is inclusive, reaching into the community. One section
of the document, "Roles and Responsibilities," describes the roles and
responsibilities of parents/guardians and technical and administrative
staff (including the eighteen newly created language arts/reading spe-
cialist positions). It also includes collaborative efforts with "universities and community agencies, including tutoring programs to help
parents in their reading interactions and use of strategies with their
children and extra help services for students in before- and after-school
care programs offered in the schools or by various organizations." The
effort is coordinated, consistent, and connected across the living day.
Each party knew what the others were doing, and this created a unified and overtly connected set of related experiences for the students.
We found that the successful programs in other places, such as Hudson
and King Middle Schools and International High School, followed similarly well-coordinated efforts. At Hudson, for instance, Hope Anderson, assistant superintendent for curriculum, said:

> We have worked very hard to develop a set of goals. . . . It's not
> my goals so much as what we can develop as a team. That
> doesn't mean I don't have any. What it means is that my ideas
> become stronger as I hear others think. So we really begin to say
> what we mean as we question one another.

In the typical schools, however, this was not the case. Instead,
individual teachers made isolated decisions based on a range of factors
at their disposal. Mechanisms that encourage coordination across
classes or grades lacked support or were absent. During our first year
at Tawasentha High School, for example, individual teachers instituted
changes on their own. Margaret Weiss incorporated into her classroom
the rich writing and thinking activities that she had learned from summer workshops. However, these changes, although extremely well

intended and executed, were not made in response to a larger, programwide perceived need, and so they stopped at her classroom door. The instructional foci and the skills and knowledge that the students were expected to learn differed dramatically in the two English classes we studied at Tawasentha. There was no coordinated effort to plan, develop, or review either curriculum or instruction at either the district or school level. During the first year of our study, the English teachers at Tawasentha did not interact, collaborate, or coordinate their instructional efforts, nor did they interact about ways to improve instruction.

Fostering Teacher Participation in Professional Communities

Another important characteristic of the successful English programs we studied is the extent to which teachers and administrators are members of a number of communities that sustain them in their efforts. Louis, Marks, and Kruse's (1996) study of within-school communities and McLaughlin and Talbert's (1993) study of math collaboratives emphasize the importance of professional community not only on the personal and intellectual lives of teachers but also on students. Our study, focusing on the range of professional communities teachers experience, permitted us to follow the variety of professional communities that nourished teachers across our two-year study. We saw administrative and teaching colleagues invite each other into a range of communities at the school, district, and state levels. Participating in these communities was part of the social milieu.

All the teachers we studied in the effective programs were members of several ongoing professional communities (e.g., teams and support groups, curriculum development groups, local reading groups, English and reading affiliates, university-school collaborations) that gave them ideas and nourished them in their daily efforts as well as in their grand plans. They also had personal networks that fed into their professional knowledge and interests and provided feedback from a range of perspectives. These networks existed in many different arenas—e.g., national, professional, state, university, local, district, and school (departments and/or teams)—and were collegial as well as social. Individual teachers participated in different communities, but whichever they chose, these communities gave them people with whom they could plan and work through problems. The teachers in the effective programs did not feel they were alone; there was always someone nearby to dream with and commiserate with, and they passed on this sense of community to their students.

Community is the common thread, but what those communities are and how the teachers interacted within them differs. There was no one predominant set of networks that seemed to pervade these effective environments; rather, what seemed to make the difference was the teachers' opportunity to select from a variety of networks to find the ones that worked best for them. For example, in some cases, cross-disciplinary teams had taken the lead as the major on-site collegial networks, but where they had, disciplinary networks were almost always sought out as well to offer grounding in curriculum and achievement.

At Hudson Middle School, cross-disciplinary teams met daily. They focused in depth on students' well-being and academic progress and also sometimes developed collaborative efforts across subject areas. In addition, all language arts teachers at each grade level met on a scheduled weekly basis. However, the English teachers sometimes also met before school "to plan and to connect." Team planning time was built into Hudson's school schedule, as it was in all the more successful schools, though the frequency of these scheduled times differed from school to school, ranging from once a week to daily.

At Miami Edison High School, after seeing a particularly interesting lesson in a colleague's class and asking her about the idea, Kathy Humphrey explained:

> I combined what I learned in a pilot program with what a colleague taught me about reading strategies. I've had a positive experience with my colleagues. And I get lots of support from [administration]. I need a group of English teachers to work with.

At International High School, the faculty worked in "big idea" interdisciplinary teams that created curriculum, arranged schedules for students and teachers, and developed projects for assessing student performance. Thus the teachers interacted on a daily basis, with many opportunities to reflect on their own practice, students' progress, and new ideas. The principal said that the many student teachers and interns who worked with them were one of the important ways in which new ideas became points of conversation for the entire team. Overall, an "incredible amount of professional community . . . is . . . built into the schoolwide system." When Marsha Slater became concerned that her team needed to focus more heavily on the students' literacy development, she brought it to the group. Although it took many months of discussion, a plan was worked out. In addition to their self-selected teaching teams, all the teachers at International belonged to peer evaluation teams wherein, periodically in their career, they reviewed and were reviewed by each other. The teachers themselves maintained portfolios with self-evaluations, peer evaluations, reflections, goals, and progress statements.[1]

The effective teachers we studied also belonged to professional organizations and read professional journals. Each was active in one or more of the organizations to which they belonged, attending conferences, and also presenting. They usually went to the conferences with colleagues they knew, and they met others there. An integral part of their conference life involved discussing concerns facing the field, new ideas, and approaches in curriculum, instruction, or assessment. For instance, Gloria Rosso and Cathy Starr of Hudson Middle School attended an annual conference of the National Council of Teachers of English, as did their department chair. At the convention, they not only met with us about the project but also attended many sessions, some alone and some together. Both at the conference and after they returned home, they discussed the ideas they found interesting and relevant to their own situations. Each was also active at the state and local levels, where once again they not only organized and presented, but also used the time to gather ideas to carry back for professional exchange within their districts and schools.[2]

In addition to these more formal networks, we also found a variety of informal ones. Every one of the teachers we studied had at least one colleague at school, or someone who taught elsewhere, or an interested significant other, with whom to share joys, agonies, and ideas that affect instructional plans, decisions, and actions. Each had contact with individuals who made a difference in the ways they thought about their subject, their students, and themselves as professionals. Through these interactions they confronted philosophical as well as more superficial differences, learned from and challenged each other, and developed their own voices. Take Rita Gold and Susan Gropper at Highland Oaks Middle School, for example. Each said the other was her most important colleague. Not only were they members of the same faculty, but they held theoretical views in common. Louis, Marks, and Kruse (1996) suggest that shared norms and values are important elements of a schoolwide professional community. Gold and Gropper had grown together as professionals, with each other as well as with the Miami-Dade County English language arts faculty. They collaborated on projects and planned and developed materials for lessons they taught separately. About their relationship, Gold said:

> I knew Susan before I transferred [to Highland Oaks]. . . . I think we're both on the same wavelength. There's time for creativity,

but the basics must be included. When we work on a unit together, like the literature circles, we bounce off one another. . . . We work better together than on our own. . . . When I moved to ninth grade, Susan shared everything she had with me. . . . We're friends outside of school and have been for many years. She's on my list of top ten teachers I'd love my nephews to have as a teacher. . . . I feel the same way about her as about the people uptown [district English language arts staff].

Gropper said, "[Rita's] creativity and outgoing personality are a perfect match to my more left-brained approach. Together we created units that still prompt a smile. . . . Just talking to each other always generates ideas or concerns that delight and surprise us."[3]

The administrators, too, felt the necessity for participating in communities and saw their importance in ongoing professional growth. Marina Garcia was the principal of King Middle School during the first year and a half of our study; she was later promoted to districtwide assistant superintendent for curriculum and instruction. While at King, she had been a highly collaborative principal, having organized a variety of formal and informal teams, committees, and lunchtime working groups. She and Vera Coleman, the superintendent of schools, had co-written the proposal for state funds to create the dual language program we were studying. To do this, they brought groups of colleagues together to read, research, and conceptualize ways in which such a program could work most effectively. The program itself followed the team collaborative structure instituted in the school and added the additional programmatic community as well. From its inception, the program was to be not merely collaborative, but communal, involving within-group goals, sharing, and articulation. After its inception, Garcia remained a member of this community, along with many others. Thus, when she arrived in her new office in the central administration building, she was dismayed to see that there was no room for people to meet. She said, "How can I get things going and make change without at least a round table where people can discuss and work ideas, and become a community?" She then led us into a nearby room to show us where her new office, with ample "people space," was being installed.

Another example is the principal of Highland Oaks Middle School, who had been the assistant principal until our study began. His teachers had begun to organize into critical friends groups with their colleagues, with the support of the previous principal. He had supported their efforts because he felt it his job to do so, "but I was thinking, this isn't really going to do anything. But we're going to do it. The boss [the previous principal] wants to do it. . . . But I slowly felt changes." As his involvement increased, he voiced a growing appreciation for professional communities of his own:

> I'm more of a nuts-and-bolts person. . . . I'm not much into the feelings of education experience. We went to a thing this summer for national school reform faculty, and we went to a weeklong session. I learned what a critical friends group is all about. My critical friends group is a high school principal in Seattle, a high school principal in California, and a middle school principal in Texas. She and I talk all the time [by e-mail]—the guy in Seattle all the time too. . . . What we do as administrators, we bounce [ideas] off each other. . . . I came back really rejuvenated. . . . I had the best time . . . and really learned a lot about protocols, and being able to work through problems with colleagues, and understanding how to give hot and cold criticism, and all that good stuff.

About his teachers' experiences with critical friends groups, he said, "What it's done for this faculty, is just given them more of a feeling of being on the cutting edge of a new reform that's going on nationwide. That they're a part of it. And now the critical friends group is an avenue for them to talk about it."

In turn, students in these schools became part of a community of learners, with people to turn to for knowledge and support. They had a sense of themselves as learners, responsible for their own choices and progress. Again the principal:

> [They're] just opening their classrooms a lot more. Not just to other teachers, but also letting the kids feel much more a part of classes, as opposed to the way I was going through this school: you're sitting there and hearing the teacher. Now it's group work, projects. You know . . . put it in the lap of the kids.

Kathy Humphrey spent a great deal of time at the beginning of each school year helping her students at Miami Edison High School learn to listen to each other, work together, appreciate the various perspectives and knowledge others bring, and become a community of learners. Throughout the year, she reorganized her room so that students could sit at group tables for the frequent small-group work or put their chairs into a semicircle to enable maximum interaction during whole-class discussion groups. This procedure was echoed in all of the classrooms in our more successful schools, even when class space was in short supply.

When asked about why she thought there was such an unusual degree of agreement in theoretical views across the teachers with whom we worked in Miami-Dade County, English Language Arts Director Bossard said, "Everyone within the [county supervisory] team works together. We create and brainstorm together. From the beginning, we relied on each other." And Sallie Snyder, the secondary school English language arts supervisor in Miami-Dade County, said, "It isn't one person's vision. We work together. We know what good teaching looks like. We've melded our philosophies into one workable paradigm . . . [with] a high level of trust and respect; each person knows that someone else knows or can do something better than themselves. In general, all of us consider that sort of collaborative effort crucial in reaching our desired goals."

Both administrators saw themselves as part of a much larger community effort, one that started before them and will carry on after they leave. Layers of history, past and present, continue, as with family.

It is too easy to assume that, once in place, these communities simply sustain themselves. Here is an e-mail from Karis MacDonnell of Ruben Dario Middle School, in mid-January 1998, soon after her winter break:

> I have been discontented with things in general lately and have been wondering why. I realized that I wasn't teaching [at the college] first semester and I wasn't doing as much reading or exchanging as many ideas with others as usual. I think I have neglected to reflect! Over the holidays I had to plan and write a new (for me) course in curriculum for elementary teachers— that got my brain going! Then I had some conversations with my mentor. My course started, student teacher arrived full-time, and Tanya [Manning, field researcher] arrived, and all of a sudden I'm having professional conversations with myself and others again.
>
> I feel much better about myself & my teaching now! Isn't that weird? Just a couple of months of "isolation" and I could tell the difference. . . . But it also made me think about colleagues who NEVER do the things I neglected to do that got me off track. They must feel terrible about themselves and their profession. But, they don't realize what they're missing. . . .

Louis, Marks, and Kruse (1996) describe professional communities in part as places where not only collaboration, but also what they call "deprivatized practice," occurs. While these elements typify the more successful programs we studied, teachers' experiences were vastly different in the typical schools, where professional communities were virtually absent. Resources to support teacher participation were often lacking. Even when school and district groups were formed, they lacked the essential professional support. During the first year of our study at Tawasentha, for example, we learned that the teachers rarely discussed professional issues. Lunch talk, even for those teachers who ate together, rarely focused on discussion of ideas or activities in the field. The newly instituted social studies and English cross-disciplinary efforts stimulated little collaborative planning and discourse, with parallel rather than coordinated curriculum and instruction (see Adler & Flihan [1997] for more information about parallel and coordinated curriculum and instruction). Further, the English teachers rarely met as a department—just twice a year, and then "only for business that must get done." We saw no coordination or sharing of ideas. Margaret Weiss wanted to grow professionally and wanted colleagues with whom to discuss ideas, but found no one at Tawasentha. Nicole Scott, on the other hand, showed little interest in changing her preferred practices, and seemed unaware that her old standbys were not working. She said she had attended conferences and workshops, some by choice and some mandated. "They sort of rejuvenate you and give you some new ideas . . . an opportunity to interact with colleagues. . . . I came away with a couple of good writing assignments [from Nancie Atwell] that I still use." However, for a planned observation, for instance, she had her students engage in a vocabulary lesson, listening to a commercially prepared reel-to-reel tape recording of words being read in succession both in and out of sentences. They were to mark the correct definitions in their accompanying workbooks. There was no discussion of the meanings in larger contexts nor of etymological clues to look for. During this work time, Scott helped students make selection decisions when they seemed to need help. She did not offer instruction about ways to understand what the words meant or how they could be used. After the lesson, she remarked that the vocabulary program had been one of her favorite activities for many years. She did not reflect on her students' compliant—but lack of cognitive—engagement with the task. When asked about interaction with colleagues, she said, "There's not a lot of time in the school day for interaction."

This atmosphere of noncollaboration began to change during the second year. A consultant was brought into the English department as a change agent, with the goal of raising expectations as well as achievement. She was a local university professor charged with stimulating the teachers to read, critique, and contemplate ways to improve students' performance. Department meetings were reinstituted. After several months, the quality of professional interaction rose substantially during these meetings. Professional ideas that the teachers had read or heard about during the past ten years began to surface, and inquiry into effective practice was beginning. During the second year, what Nicole Scott talked to us about when we visited, such as her teaching style, began to change. She incorporated more writing process and interactive activities in her classroom. She said, "When I've tried collaborative writing, they seem more intent on revising the piece than when they're working on a piece by themselves."

Creating Activities That Offer Teachers a Sense of Agency

A third characteristic of the successful programs we studied is that the participants had an ongoing sense of agency; they could effect change. The teachers in these programs all felt they could shape the kind of work they did: they developed curriculum; solved problems; made decisions and set directions in curriculum and instruction in their department, school, or district; helped choose new colleagues. They passed this sense of purposeful action on to their students. Each of the schools had adopted at least some components of school-based management and shared decision making. In fact, Miami-Dade County was one of the first school systems in the nation to decentralize (Fiske, 1991). They decided the key to better schools was the professionalization of teachers, providing them with a sense of ownership of and responsibility for what goes on in their schools. We saw the teachers in Miami-Dade County initiate their own proposals with administration support, and collaborate on those initiated by other teachers and administrators, with full confidence that if granted they would be enacted in ways that were compatible with the teachers' goals. Agency was given and accepted. For example, in October of our first year, Rita Gold wrote the following e-mail,

> I just came from a DCCTE [Dade County Council of Teachers of English] meeting. Susan [Gropper] and I spent all day in the conference room writing for the Blue Ribbon School of Excellence application. We'll be out of class on Wednesday too. Since Friday is a teacher workday, that pretty much messes up the week.

Rita Gold and Susan Gropper and their principal felt their contribution to the application was important and that their efforts could help the school earn an award they all considered important. That same October, Kathy Humphrey of Miami Edison High School wrote:

> I have something for you to look over. I wrote a proposal to support the testing results for both the Florida Writes! Exam and

HSCT [High School Competency Test]. The state, I guess, mandated that an allocation of $10 per student be given to the Education Excellence Committee to spend in support of the school improvement plan. That means a nice chunk that could allow us to do something differently. So here we go! The following is my vision of what it could be. . . .

Similarly, International High School was founded on an ethic of professional cooperation. The entire staff shared major administrative responsibilities through a committee structure. The Staff Development Committee planned and oversaw the inservice staff development program. The Faculty Planning Personnel Committee interviewed and selected new staff members and administered the peer evaluation program.

The teachers in these effective schools were also involved in curriculum development. In many cases this was a continuing activity that involved selecting crosscutting themes and relevant instructional material and activities. This was especially true in schools with extensive cross-disciplinary programs, such as King Middle School, Turner Tech, and International High School. Whether the teachers were involved in developing lessons for cross-disciplinary efforts or planning ways to offer the high-level instruction that was most appropriate for their students, their decisions shaped important aspects of their curriculum and instructional offerings.

Not only were the teachers given agency, but they assumed it in response to their own desire to change. For example, Chris Kirchner co-wrote and received an Annenberg Foundation two-year grant to start critical friends groups at Turner Tech. The money was earmarked for paying substitutes so that the groups of teachers could meet no less than once a month. Kirchner was fully encouraged by her principal. The critical friends groups, once in place, were further contributors to the entire faculty's sense of agency. Beyond this, Kirchner wrote proposals and received a number of small grants to develop instructional activities and approaches. These were well received by the district, and she was invited to share her work at district workshops. She and colleagues were also given a sense of agency by the district when they were invited to help write competencies for the newly developing competency-based curriculum. Their work had a real effect not only on what their own students studied, but also on what all the students in the district were exposed to. In fact, Kirchner said the competencies were written specifically enough yet broadly enough to provide a common set of instructional goals without denying teachers agency or creativity to achieve the goals in ways that worked for themselves and their students.[4]

It is this ethic—that one's effort will be useful, will lead to some end—that permeated the teachers' lives and gave them purpose. This sense of agency extended to all levels within the school community, from the central office to the teachers to the students. International High School's Handbook states:

> Committee membership [by the faculty] is crucial to our teaching approach. It enables teachers to experience the collaborative process that they expect of their students. They can more readily serve as role models.[5]

Collaborative work and inquiry learning were at the center of classroom approaches in the effective schools we studied. In literature, for example, the students were given responsibility for developing, explaining, and defending their interpretations, even as they were supported by needed instruction from the teacher. Karis MacDonnell (Ruben Dario Middle School) gave the following assignment on *The Yearling* by Marjorie Kinnan Rawlings:

> Sometimes a particular person has a strong influence on other people. There are several such characters in *The Yearling*. Think about some of the characters you are meeting in *The Yearling*. Think about the ways one person affects others in the story. Choose one of the strong characters from this book and explain how that person's influence affects others in the story.

Thus these students were asked to make their own choices and discuss them as a way to explore characterizations in greater depth. This kind of agency also pervaded MacDonnell's journalism class, where the students were the editors and assistant editors of the school newspaper. For example, one day when we entered, a student editor was using the overhead projector to make an outline of the deadlines that needed to be met. The information was being provided to her by the various editorial departments. They had a newspaper to get out and would make sure it was not merely on time, but also interesting and well written. MacDonnell's role was minimal in this moment, although her efforts to help the students become good writers were both helpful and instructive. She felt their agency motivated and sharpened their learning. What was even more surprising about the students' agency is that the editor at the time was from Nicaragua, and it was only her third year in the United States. The newspaper has won awards, and Ruben Dario has itself won many awards recognizing the school as a whole. When asked why Ruben Dario got these awards against all odds, MacDonnell said, "Because they can." It was this sense that permeated the atmosphere, and maximized achievement: the sense of giving and having agency because the participants are capable. They will do what they can and learn what they must.

Gail Slatko, also at Ruben Dario, began most lessons by developing the knowledge, understandings, and strategies that the students would need in order to carry out the new activity. Because the activity always involved problem solving and learning, she said she then became "an orchestrator. I let the kids take over and work on their own." To encourage the students to take ownership of their learning, the effective teachers we studied used aspects of personal reflection as well as peer response. They had the students react to, check, and make suggestions for their classmates' writing, both in terms of content and organization and in terms of surface features such as spelling and grammar.

At Turner Tech, students in the Academy of Finance developed their own stock portfolios and tracked them over time. Students wrote their reasons for each purchase and chronicled what they were learning. They wrote predictions about how their stocks would do and then recorded how things actually developed. One day, local stock brokers came to meet with Kirchner's class, but beforehand, the students, in small groups, had planned for the event by preparing questions, predicting what they might learn, and deciding how best to use the brokers' time to their advantage. The sense of agency developed in these schools helped students take responsibility for their own learning, motivating them as they learned how to analyze situations and then organize, plan, and take action in appropriate ways.

Circumstances in the typical schools were much different. Teachers had little sense of agency. When they worked toward change, their recommendations were rarely acknowledged or supported. Professional programs delivered services rather than encouraging teachers to determine their own needs. At Tawasentha, despite Superintendent Hatfield's support for teachers' involvement in and ownership of change, a sense of agency had not permeated the professional environment. Nor, from the teachers' point of view, was the administration fully supportive. For example, when discussing support for instructional change, Margaret Weiss spoke of the social studies and English team-teaching effort that had been instituted the prior year and in which she had participated:

> Last year, my social studies teacher and I were able to block. We blocked four days a week, and on Fridays we did normal time.

The administration supported us, and it was wonderful. We decided to move up as tenth-grade teachers to pilot the tenth-grade team to see if students would do better on the Global Studies Regents [exam] having the same teacher. Because I worked with Laura, I moved up with her. What was very disappointing is we get the mouth talk that yes, we support you and we support blocking, but the way they scheduled us, we can't block this year. And that's a disappointment to us and to the students. It's really easy to lose heart.

Valuing Commitment to Professionalism

The fourth characteristic of the effective programs we studied is the pervading sense of professional identity each participant displayed. They were proud to be educators, thought of themselves as professionals, and carried their professional selves with them wherever they went. They were in touch with the larger world and with the concerns of others in regard to education. They considered themselves spokespersons for the profession. Norma Bossard, English language arts director in Miami-Dade County, said:

> A characteristic of us [the language arts department] is that any of us would go back to the classroom tomorrow morning and do a good job and be happy there. We're not out because we don't want to be teachers. That's one of the things I really attribute to Zelda [Glazer, the previous language arts/reading director,] is defining the role of the department that way. I always thought they picked us because they knew we could do good staff development and remain teachers. They knew we could go back to the classroom.

It was this sense of being a teacher as well as speaking for teachers that characterized all the professionals we studied. In an interview, Glazer recalled:

> When I first got the job as supervisor, the whole setup downtown [in the central office] was different. One of the people I worked with was very smart, very knowledgeable, very current in her information. There was nothing ossified about her. But at the time everyone accepted the bureaucratic paradigm which was you didn't go into a school unless you were invited. . . . They don't want you. . . . So downtown, they were not connected to the body of the patient. And so it was a big jump when we decided that was no way to function. But getting into classrooms, being close to teachers, was my ideal. . . . The other thing that helped was the Bay Area Writing Project, the National Writing Project which was used as a model for the annual writing institute we prepare for our teachers [now renamed the Zelda

Glazer Writing Institute]. In our view it has become a learning, not just writing, institute, for everyone.

The teachers also maintained a professional stance, kept up with their fields, and continually honed their own skills. Bossard and all of the English language arts supervisors subscribed to a number of journals and magazines and expected the teachers to do the same. "We make it real important to them to join one of the organizations. . . . We let them know that's the standard—to be part of the group we've got, that you're a professional and a professional joins the professional organizations and reads the literature."

They also share their knowledge with each other. For example, Susan Gropper at Highland Oaks had adapted reciprocal teaching strategies (initially introduced into the ongoing professional discussion within the English language arts program) to improve her students' reading comprehension before they were incorporated into the new Comprehensive Reading Plan. She shared this with other teachers in the district via workshops. The effective teachers also mentored preservice teachers and new teachers. Take Cathy Starr and Gloria Rosso at Hudson Middle School as examples. Both were excellent and experienced teachers: Starr had been teaching at Hudson for twenty-six years, and Rosso had been there for six years after having taught in New York City for seventeen years. From the moment Rosso arrived, Starr assumed a professional responsibility to help her make a comfortable transition. She invited Rosso into her classroom and to presentations and workshops she was giving, both at school and at local, state, and national conferences.[6] Rosso, on the other hand, had student teachers in her classroom. With care and guidance, she helped them gain a sense not only of the curriculum, classroom organization, and instructional approaches and interactions, but also of the many complex roles an English teacher plays. Rosso served as a role model not only for her students but also for the many student teachers she cared for and helped grow as professionals.

The effective teachers we studied felt they were experts in their profession and took pleasure in sharing what they knew with others. Most of them were involved in some aspect of professional development. They taught at local colleges and were frequent speakers at conferences and workshops. Some had won teacher of the year and other excellence awards, and others were officers of professional organizations or had published in professional journals. They thought of education as a worthy and important profession and placed their professional obligations extremely high on their list of priorities.

The school administrators also treated their teachers as professionals, providing time for team and planning meetings, as well as released time with pay for professional meetings, conferences, and other professional activities, such as invitations to work on state standards or test development committees. They did this because they knew that treating their teachers as professionals would ultimately benefit the district.

While the successful programs generally exuded a professional pride, teachers in the typical schools were less likely to feel involved in their profession. The typical schools and districts did not have expectations regarding teachers' commitment to their profession, aside from their classroom duties. The teachers were certainly less activist in participating in broader changes within their department and school than were teachers in the more effective programs. They were neither invited nor encouraged to become involved. At Tawasentha, for example, during the first year of the study, Nicole Scott showed almost no awareness of the changes in English education that had taken place over the past twenty years, and she seemed unaware of the current tensions. Although Margaret Weiss tried to keep abreast of issues, she perceived herself as being alone and never assumed a strong role of professional leadership. Superintendent Hatfield believed that professionalization of teachers was a critical part of her educational reform goals. For example, she told us that when she began her job, she started a process that engaged multiple constituencies in identifying their goals for Tawasentha.

> With Goals 2000, I was able to design a focus for the district . . . a systemic reform effort that was going to begin to think about the students, first of all a student focus—looking at the fact that the students go through a system, and that the system has to be one that provides some continuity, consistency, and a focus for what you want the students to be able to do and understand when they graduate. . . . We were able to then set up building planning teams, shared decision-making teams, and when we designed the blueprint for how they would operate, the focus would be on student results. . . . The goal of those committees was to improve student results by looking at data that existed and beginning to suggest ways to improve them. They could decide anything they wanted that related to that, as long as they had gotten the data and information to make the decisions. To support the buildings I also felt we needed three support teams: curriculum, instruction, and assessment. So we began with curriculum committees. We started mostly at the elementary level because it appeared that I was going to have to be more persuasive in terms of a new vision at the secondary level. . . . Every

> year I sit down with the principals to see if there's evidence the
> project leaders truly change theory to practice. . . . There has to
> be demonstration of change in the classroom. . . . Because it
> seemed that at the high school our own could not make the
> change, I've begun to bring in outside consultants.

Margaret Weiss, who had been a member of some of these change-agent committees, including a summer committee to develop integrated social studies and English curriculum, had also invited some writing process specialists to meet with the teachers in her school. She described the superintendent as "a visionary leader" who was "aiming toward more collaborative teaching and more discovery and collaborative learning for the students." The superintendent was creating opportunities for professional discourse. The consultant who met with the English teachers provided them with opportunities to read, discuss, and develop opinions about issues and approaches. However, even in the second year, we did not see the teachers interact with each other or their fellow teachers apart from arranged meetings.

Engendering Caring Attitudes

The fifth crosscutting characteristic of these effective programs is that they share an ethos of caring (Noddings, 1984). The teachers we studied care about their students, and about the people with whom they work. In some schools, they hugged each other a lot, in others they showed affection for each other more subtly. They asked each other how things were going and went beyond small talk at the coffee machine. Miami-Dade County language arts supervisor Sallie Snyder sent a welcome-back-to-school letter to teachers at the end of the summer that began this way:

> Dear Exalted Ones,
>
> The warmest and most sincere welcome to all of you as the 1997–1998 school year begins. I need not tell you that we are also beginning year two of the "Langer Project" and with it the joys and stresses I know that brings.

The letter ends with: "My best regards and greatest admiration to all." Her jocular language notwithstanding, the teachers knew Snyder cared about them, appreciated them, and knew that they were involved in a professional commitment that cost them—in time and comfort. The letter was one small act of caring among countless others.

The teachers appreciated expressions of caring and extended this ethos to their interactions with students. For example, Pedro

Méndez, from King Middle School, said about his Spanish-proficient students in the dual language program:

> Kids need to be comfortable. They need to see me as a resource and I hope that's what's happening. Not only that they see me as an authoritative figure, that they see me as a mentor, as a role model. When I walk out in the hall, they can say, "Well, that's Mr. Méndez. He's my teacher. He's what I would like to be when I grow up."

When he taught, Méndez maintained a very caring attitude toward his students in the way he looked at them, tried to draw them out, and guided them to engage with the topics being taught. Once, at the end of the day, he found that something had been taken from his office. He didn't need the item, and he could easily have ignored the incident. Instead, he questioned others about who had been in his office, and when he thought he knew who the culprit was, he got into his car and drove to the main street, where he found the culprit. He drove the boy back to school, spoke with him, and then took him to the principal's office, explaining in a parental manner, "It isn't only important for what you did now, but you must never do something like this again."

Each effective school held team meetings where they discussed students who were absent, who might be in trouble academically, socially, or in other ways, and they tried to work out ways to help, before problems escalated. They brought students in, and families too. They went the extra mile to try to make things work, and students and parents knew it. To create a "family" feel, most of the schools adorned their entranceways and hallways with photographs of past students, field trips, and family and community members engaged in projects. Parents were encouraged to visit classrooms to become familiar with the programs and to volunteer to help. And all the schools had a range of community, parent, and teacher committees, advisory groups, and common welfare and social interest groups that created a sense of belonging.

The teachers cared about the curriculum as well as their students' learning, constantly monitored their students' grades, and were responsive to signals from their students that changes in instructional approaches or activities were needed. One of Turner Tech's standards was to help their students develop more relationships with adults, especially those in business and industry. We observed one meeting when eleven industry guests (financial planners and brokers) spent a morning with the students in the Academy of Finance. The agreement was that they would return, soon. The guests felt valued, not over-whelmed, and so did the students. Many of the brokers invited inter-ested students to contact them if they could be of help. As part of the process, the students used reflection sheets to evaluate the visitors' helpfulness to them personally.[7]

In contrast, in the typical schools, human interaction was respectful, among and between both teachers and students, but the schools lacked a deeply caring atmosphere and a unified sense of com-munity. Upon entering Tawasentha, one saw that the walls were bare and the hallways empty and quiet. The friendly interactions, the evi-dence of class projects and activities, and the immediate sense of the school's inhabitants were all absent. This was not the case in Weiss's classroom, where warm interactions and questions about how stu-dents were feeling were the norm. Scott, however, remained a more distant teacher, holding herself more apart. The constant student-case discussions and team efforts that prevailed at the other schools also seemed absent; problems were dealt with in other ways. During the second year, Scott told us about the faculty room:

> We decided to personalize it, and we all brought in artificial flowers just to make it look less sterile. . . . At the end of the year we do a camping day, just the female members. And we do sometimes talk about work, but we just have a good time too. Over winter break there's a group going to the culinary institute in my car for the day.

While this is not a bad thing, these teachers kept their interac-tions at a social level, rather than using their growing friendships in ways that focused on their students' learning needs or experiences.

Fostering Respect for Learning

Lastly, the teachers we studied in the successful schools were learners themselves, in their personal as well as their professional lives. They were truly the lifelong learners they want their students to become. For instance, Donald Silvers, a teacher in King Middle School's dual lan-guage program, said, "Well, growing up, some of my family members were teachers. I've always respected teaching as a profession. I always liked school. I had a positive, very positive school career. I love going to classes. I love learning."

The teachers were offered a plethora of opportunities to keep in touch with the latest thinking in their field. More than any single type of learning activity, it seemed that what typified this feature for excellence was the range of opportunities and the manner in which teachers were invited to intellectually engage with and respond to the ideas. Each district invited guest speakers and consultants to interact with the teachers. Someone, be it a curriculum supervisor, department chair, principal, or fellow teacher, duplicated and shared pertinent journal articles. In class, talk about learning pervaded their days. Their students joined in the conversation, talked about their own learning, and shared it with each other; they considered themselves learners too.

The effective teachers learned to be computer literate, and almost all had access to computers either in their own classroom or in a media center. The least computer-rich schools were in the process of increasing their capacity. While the teachers valued the Internet, they made use of it in their classes only after they saw how it could enhance their students' learning. Gloria Rosso, for instance, taught a research unit on names. The students were learning to use a variety of materials to research the history of their first and last names. In addition to the many books on surnames and first names she had brought into her classroom, she also taught her students how to use the Internet to research genealogies. Each student developed his or her own genealogy, but they shared knowledge about how to get the information, use the technology, and gain research skills. In another instance, Shawn DeNight was selected as one of a few teachers in the United States to visit the Ukraine as part of an educators team. He brought letters from his students to the students he would meet and planned to encourage a letter exchange across the countries. As effective teachers, these educators understood that students must learn to use computer technology both as a developing skill and for the resources it makes available. A group of Miami-Dade County teachers participated in a district-sponsored, hands-on workshop on using the World Wide Web. One of our field researchers found them

> enthusiastically cautious about the possibilities for Internet applications in their classrooms, concerned about how they will teach their students to discriminate among the sources available to them, how the students will learn to extract and categorize the available information, how they will learn to weave their information into a coherent whole, how to teach proper citations from electronic databases, and the need for appropriate higher literacy skills.

Even as they aired their concerns and, for the moment, kept Internet use on the back burner, they were constructive in assessing its potentials.

Beyond inservices and other professional development offered to them, these teachers attended conferences and meetings, took courses, and belonged to groups. The topics they engaged dealt not only with education but also with a range of issues and ideas that help them grow as individuals. In Miami-Dade County, for example, teachers were given inservice credit for participating in adult readers' groups. Here, teachers met in people's homes on a rotating basis and talked about books that had been selected by the participants. Director Norma Bossard believed that love of reading was infectious, and that "some of it will rub off on the children." Describing one such group, ninth-grade teacher Susan Gropper said:

> Last Friday our [teacher] reading group met to discuss *The Color of Water*. What fun it was to share our interpretations, complaints, praise, and personal experiences. I enjoyed telling my students about it in the hope that they might be inspired to discover the pleasure of reading and sharing themselves.

Not only did this activity offer an opportunity for teachers across the disciplines to get to know each other, it sometimes also engaged them in discussing content and strategies they might share with their students. Using this model, Rita Gold had developed a very popular and well-attended Borders Book Club for Highland Oaks middle-grade students.

In their professional learning, the teachers placed themselves in the stream of new knowledge in their field, and weighed and reworked ideas in ways that made sense for their students. Shawn DeNight, for example, attended Miami-Dade County's two-week summer writing institute, an intensive and highly empowering informal mixture of speakers, workshops, and sharing. He said:

> The Writing Institute, for me, is like a banquet where I just feast. . . . You always hear new people, and it's just time to sit and reflect, and talk about the way you teach. I mean, I remember just two years ago, we thought about creating our own little mini-writing institute here at Edison for teachers in other departments. We called it the Edison Model Institute, and we had some of the various presenters from the writing institute come, and then our teachers taught other teachers, just to promote reading and writing in the classroom. So I do think they have that influence. You know, I've benefited from them.

DeNight often used models in his classroom: "What better way to make things concrete than to use models?" Thus, when he saw some poems used as models in a summer writing institute workshop, he knew they would work for his own class. Using poems from the workshop, as well as others he himself had chosen, he developed a unit that introduced poems and some of the literary elements such as imagery, simile, alliteration, and personification that made the poems work. Using the poems they studied as models, the students wrote their own poetry and served as peer editors. After much feedback on several drafts, they proudly keyed their poems into the computer and printed them out. As with the other effective teachers we studied, DeNight chose ideas that he felt could help him reach his own goals for student achievement, that fit into his curriculum, and that could be shaped to fit his teaching approach.

The effective teachers let their students know when they were using what they had learned in their professional development. For example, Gail Slatko said to her class as she began a writing activity, "You remember the writing course I told you about that I took this summer. This is something I learned."

As students, the teachers also reflected on themselves in the role of learner and gained new ideas for their own teaching. DeNight told us that for several years he had been taking a carpentry course. He told his students about the course and his progress with what he was building at the time. He said:

> One day it hit me, that as a student in that class I was learning about activity theory. You know, what it's like to be a learner in a real activity setting and what it does for how you understand things. And so I told my class about it and how we needed to work with activities too, and they'd see the difference.

In contrast, typical schools did not usually make teachers' learning overt, nor did they provide students with opportunities to see adults enthusiastically involved as learners. During the first year at Tawasentha, we saw little evidence that teachers were engaged as learners, either in professional or in personal endeavors. If they did engage in such activities, they did not share them with their students or colleagues. By the second year of participation, Tawasentha had many parts in place but was still far from the cohesive learning community Jane Hatfield wanted so much to foster. But this too was beginning to change. When she began as superintendent, professional development had not been a focus at Tawasentha—neither professional days for conferences nor invited speakers. Occasionally articles were distributed. By the end of our two years there, the teachers were reading a variety of books and articles and interacting about the ideas. A consultant was meeting with the teachers on a monthly basis, engaging in book talks about professional books and articles and discussing instructional approaches and activities. The teachers were beginning to act as learners, to overtly seek professional knowledge and share their own ideas with each other.

Overall, Hatfield was doing a great deal to change the sociocognitive context of the school district, affecting ideas and images of change by developing overlapping communities of professionals and parents to look beyond the usual—to read, research, discuss, and also set new goals and processes. Her leadership encompassed the characteristics we have seen at work in the more successful schools. And by the end of our project, changes in goals as well as performance had begun to appear. She assured us she planned to keep "plugging and pushing. . . . Matter of fact, in the next five years we'll see a tremendous change in the high school."

Conclusion

It is important to remember that it is the six characteristics working in concert that seem to mark the difference between the effective and typical schools; every school we studied that was performing better than comparable ones exhibited all six characteristics:

1. coordinating efforts to improve achievement,
2. fostering teacher participation in professional communities,
3. creating activities that provide teachers with a sense of agency,
4. valuing commitment to professionalism,
5. engendering caring attitudes, and
6. fostering respect for learning.

These characteristics can be observed more specifically in the school portraits you will read in Chapters 4 through 6.

4 Effective Teachers in an Urban District

Steven D. Ostrowski
Central Connecticut State University

*W*hen those of us involved in the Excellence in English (EIE) project began interviewing and studying effective language arts teachers in Miami-Dade County, Florida, we sensed we had tapped a gold mine. The teachers were outstanding and were helping their students, most of whom live in poor, urban communities, perform better than similar students in other districts. In addition, we heard over and over again from the teachers about the substantial support they received from the county's Division of Language Arts/Reading. They talked about their contacts with the division in glowing terms, calling the staff "educational giants," "role models," "fairy godmothers," "my vitamin B shots." One veteran teacher told us that the district staff "consistently presents meaningful and stimulating inservices on a wide variety of subjects, from improving test scores to the latest techniques for improving reading, to portfolio preparation." Another said, "All my writing instruction techniques came from what I learned in district workshops, either directly from one of the language arts supervisors or from a colleague who attended a writing workshop." Still another said that the staff "give me the stimulus I need. They're curriculum-based and have patents on presenting the best workshops. If I ever stopped interacting with them, I know I would suffer terribly, and so would my students."

All of the features of teachers' professional lives that I discussed in Chapter 3 come to life in the Dade County Division of Language Arts/Reading environment.

As you've read in the previous chapters, the English language arts program in Miami-Dade County is highly professional and blessed with some outstanding teachers. This chapter provides a portrait of four of those teachers: Chris Kirchner, Janas Masztal, Rita Gold, and Susan Gropper. It brings to life what "English" means to them, and how what happens in their classes is helping students to become more highly literate. The chapter begins with a brief general description of the two schools in which the teachers work.

The Schools

Despite significant differences in their student populations and missions, both William H. Turner Technical Arts High School and Highland Oaks Middle School deserve to be considered excellent, indeed effective, schools—schools that are making positive differences in the lives of the students who attend them. In both cases, for different reasons and in different ways, these schools are "beating the odds."

At the time of this study, Turner was just four years old. Located in Miami's inner city, the school is surrounded by blight and economic and social depression, yet it is a multi-award-winning technical arts high school. A visitor can immediately sense that Turner is an unusual environment, an inner-city educational oasis, a place of real learning and real excitement about learning, a place of true caring and of educational pride. A visitor's subsequent visits only confirm these initial impressions. From the administrators to the teachers to the students to the security guards, there is a palpable sense at Turner that virtually *everybody* is invested in the educational enterprise, which in fact was deliberately emphasized by the founders of the school. That is, all staff are to be considered equally invested in the success of the school. As one teacher put it, "That's why the security guards here take their jobs as seriously as the principal." It is not only outcomes, in the form of rising test scores and numbers of graduates, that matter at Turner (although they matter a great deal), but the larger educational *context* as well, from the aggressively positive attitudes of those who work and study at Turner to the nearly immaculate physical appearance of the school, inside and out. Finally, the entire, complex, multilayered *process* of educating young minds, hearts, and souls matters to the staff at Turner. That process involves a great deal of meaningful interaction between administration and faculty, faculty and faculty, faculty and students, and students and students, within and beyond the classroom and even the school walls.

The curriculum at Turner is an integrated one in which students and teachers are assigned to one of seven academies: Agriscience, Applied Business Technology, Finance, Health, Industrial Technology, Broadcasting, and Residential Construction. Turner offers what it calls a "two-for-one" diploma, whereby students can earn a traditional diploma that qualifies them for entrance into two- or four-year colleges while simultaneously completing state-certified career training.

Highland Oaks, for many years among Miami's most prestigious middle schools, has long served a mostly white, middle- and upper-middle-class clientele. In recent years, however, the Highland

Oaks demographic makeup has changed significantly. The school has become more ethnically and racially diverse and includes many more students from less privileged socioeconomic backgrounds than in previous times, including many recent immigrants to the United States. Despite these challenging demographic changes, Highland Oaks continues to be a place of high energy, of engagement and involvement at all levels. The administration, faculty, students, and staff care deeply that Highland Oaks remain an excellent school. In order to do so, it has, in many ways, become a cutting-edge school.

The Teachers

By way of introduction to the four teachers and their classroom settings, the following are brief, impressionistic portraits of each of the teachers. The purpose of these portraits is to create for the reader a general sense of the individuals who have been identified as effective English teachers. Later, each of the teachers is described in greater and more specific detail, particularly as she is seen "in action" with her students.

Chris Kirchner, Eleventh- and Twelfth-Grade English/Language Arts Teacher at Turner Tech

The first time I walked into Chris Kirchner's English classroom in Turner's Academy of Finance, she was wearing antlers. Her classroom was lit not from above by the fluorescent ceiling lights, but instead by an eclectic array of lamps that Kirchner had brought into the room to create a more homey, mellow atmosphere. On the walls and boards were notes, posters, and educational messages, including the basic tenets of the Coalition of Essential Schools (Sizer, 1984).[1] One poster read *Claim*, *Data*, *Warrant* (three words that play a vital role in Kirchner's classroom, as will be shown later).

That first brief meeting took place on a mild South Florida December afternoon. Kirchner's twenty-eight students were seated around her in groups of three and four. The whole class was discussing—in an extremely lively manner, as if something both immensely important and rather fun were taking place—certain grammatical aspects of an anonymous student's essay that was projected onto a screen on a side wall. It was obvious that these students seemed genuinely to enjoy the exchanges that were taking place about grammar—about what was effective and what was not particularly effective with regard to the anonymous student author's use of language, syntax, and vocabulary. At one point Kirchner asked the students a question that she would ask many times throughout the year, a question that embodied one of her chief motivational strategies and that had to do with how the students would fare in the "real world"; the question was whether or not a certain sentence construction used in the paper being examined would go over well with employers or college admissions officers. "No way," was the response of the chorus. "Okay," she said, "so give us a better way to do it." Numerous suggestions followed.

It should be noted that Kirchner was in no way advocating that her students simply give the powers-that-be what they want. Rather, in her evocations of the "real world," she consistently attempted to balance an ideology of empowerment with strong doses of practicality. In this case, she believed that students with a wide repertoire of linguistic options stood a better chance of attaining personal goals *and* of effecting social change than would students with more limited linguistic abilities and strategies.

Leaving the room that day, I was already anxious to go back to find out if the few moments of the lesson I'd just observed were somehow a fluke or if this slightly wacky woman and her predominantly poor Black and Hispanic students (who were juniors that year) could and would sustain this kind of energy for learning over the long haul. Two years later I could honestly report that Kirchner's classes not only are consistently engaging, but that the great majority of her students have continued to develop their skills as readers, writers, speakers, and thinkers. If, like many of their peers from the inner city, they entered high school with little sense of their own potential, they left it with a great deal more.

Kirchner herself is a force not only within her classroom but within her school and district, where she is a frequent contributor to the ongoing functioning of both. Also, because of her active involvement on the national level in the Coalition of Essential Schools movement, she is a force for improving the educational future of the United States itself.

Janas Masztal, Tenth- and Eleventh-Grade English/Language Arts Teacher at Turner Tech

In order to visit Janas Masztal's English class in the Agriscience Academy at Turner Tech, one has to walk out of the airy, pastel-colored main building, cross a well-maintained parking lot dotted with palm trees, pass by several long rows of barns and stalls where animals and fowl are kept and cared for by agriscience students and faculty, cross a canal via a fenced pedestrian bridge, walk through a field of grass, and finally enter Masztal's portable classroom. The trip is not only pleasant (and quite unusual, given that this is an inner city setting), it is also well worth it from the standpoint of an observer's coming to understand what truly effective English teaching can look like.

Janas Masztal is casual, understated, ironic, and perhaps (befitting the academy she teaches in) a bit "earthy." Her rapport with her students, however, is as strong and intense in its own way as Kirchner's is with hers. There is a kind of big-sister feel to Masztal's relationship with her students. She knows their lives, their interests, their strengths and weaknesses as students of English and as young adults growing up in a troubled inner city. As her students silently read works of their choice, including newspapers and magazines, for the first fifteen minutes of the one hour-and-fifty-minute block, Masztal "visits," kneeling beside individual students, asking how things are going in math, or how the sick cow did overnight, or what a student is reading and how he or she is enjoying it. Masztal is convinced that sustained silent reading has helped make readers out of many affirmed nonreaders.

Like Kirchner, Masztal is an innovative, seemingly intrinsically motiv*ed* as well as motiv*ating*, and highly effective teacher. She particularly favors the idea of major projects as creators of curricular momentum for herself and her classes. One such project, which she ran in conjunction with a history teacher in the Agriscience Academy, was based on the theme "What is America?" (further discussed below, as well as in greater detail elsewhere [Ostrowski, 1999]).

As many interviews with them over the course of two years revealed, Masztal's students, like Kirchner's, are convinced that the learning they do in her English class, as well as the variety of ways in which that learning is accomplished, really matter to their lives; they know that it matters in the present and that it will matter in the future. As one student explained, "She teaches us a lot about English, about books and writing, you know, and how to communicate with your boss . . . because you need English for everything. English is life!"

Rita Gold, Ninth-Grade English/Language Arts Teacher at Highland Oaks Middle School

One of the human dynamos that keep Highland Oaks Middle School vibrant and ever on the educational cutting edge, despite its continually changing demographics, is longtime though still youthful English teacher, Rita Gold. Gold teaches ninth graders at the attractive suburban middle school (the Highland Oaks grade structure is 7 to 9 as opposed to the more common 6 to 8.) Essentially heterogeneously grouped, Gold's ninth graders vary widely in academic ability.

Gold's classes are places of innovative ideas in action. Students often work in small groups—for example, in literature circles—where each member of the group has a specific role with specific responsibilities. ("They like to be the 'expert' at something," Gold says.) Students also give presentations of various kinds, they "deconstruct" films, and of course they do a good deal of reading, conversing, and writing. Through all of this, Gold's persona is one of an older, wiser friend whom students know is doing everything she can to help them do well, but more than that, who is trying to bring them to truly come to love literary life as she does.

Along with her colleague and close friend Susan Gropper, Gold is a voracious idea hunter. She is always on the lookout for new ways of teaching, new materials to use, new methods to try that make sense for her students. She takes ideas from the people at the county district office, from other teachers, from journals such as *English Journal*, and tailors them to the needs of her students. Her deeply grounded knowledge of and concern for her ninth graders and their potentialities and typical resistances, the depth and breadth of her own reading, and her active involvement in professional activities in her school and on the district level enable her to create a classroom environment that is consistently stimulating to students and that helps produce meaningful, tangible learning for the entire range of the learners in her charge.

Susan Gropper, Ninth-Grade English/Language Arts Teacher at Highland Oaks Middle School

Just a few years from retirement, Susan Gropper virtually embodies the definition of "lifelong learner." As a teacher, she brings to her ninth-grade classes a great deal of energy, enthusiasm, and freshness, as well as a genuine love of her subject that has apparently not diminished after three decades of teaching. Like the other teachers in this study, Gropper has the ability to speak with her students about a literary work in a way that simultaneously conveys to them that she knows the work deeply and yet retains an openness to new discovery, as if she, like they, were encountering the characters and setting of a particular work of literature for the first time. The effect is to draw students into the work with her.

Like Gold, Gropper is not to be mistaken for someone who will try any new English/language arts–related idea simply for the sake of being trendy or for the sake of mere variation; in fact, she is wary of many recent educational "innovations." When she adopts a new method, it is because she believes it has real merit. If she tries something and it doesn't work, she'll make adjustments. If after adjustments it still doesn't work, she'll drop it. On the other hand, if an idea—for example the idea of reciprocal teaching, which Gropper enthusiastically adopted several years ago—makes great sense to her and works well in her classes, she'll not only employ it in her own classes, she'll also spread the word, including giving workshops to teachers in her own school and other district schools at the request of school and district administrators.

Some Important Commonalities among the Teachers

The four teachers profiled in this chapter are very different people with distinct personalities and life experiences. However, they have certain important things in common, a few of which are mentioned here in order to paint a picture of effective instruction that will be not only as complete as possible, but also as helpful as possible to other educators who might want to learn from these teachers and their various professional contexts. It is done, as well, in order to show how aspects of the larger contexts of their professional lives can directly influence what happens in their classrooms.

Influence of the District Office

All four teachers are highly influenced and aided by the Miami-Dade County District Language Arts Department (commonly referred to as "downtown") (Ostrowski, 1999), whose dedicated, innovative, and enthusiastic staff provide numerous workshops and teacher development programs, including an intensive, two-week summer writing institute that all Miami-Dade County English/language arts teachers have the opportunity to attend at least once in their careers. Many of the ideas and methodologies presented at district-sponsored professional development sessions, as well as at the summer writing institute, have been used to great effect by all four teachers in their classrooms. A few examples of ideas that originated from or were passed along in one form or another by the people "downtown" are the following: analysis of scoring rubrics in order to help students understand how best to write for the state-required Florida Writes!

Exam; graphic organizers; the modeling of poetry writing; literature circles; jigsawing; and reciprocal teaching. (More detailed examples of some of these concepts as they are actually used in the classroom are provided later in this chapter.)

According to district supervisors interviewed in the course of this study, not all teachers in Miami-Dade County take advantage of the numerous opportunities for professional development that the district offers; these four teachers usually do. Furthermore, all have, at one time or another, been invited by the district to help write curriculum, provide workshops on various methodologies and innovations, and/or co-facilitate at the summer writing institute. The four received these invitations because of their reputations in the district as hardworking, intelligent, innovative, and successful teachers. District supervisors consider these teachers valuable resources not only for their individual schools and students, but for all of Miami-Dade County.

Involvement within Their Schools

Another commonality among the teachers is that they are all active within their schools. Several are or have been department heads, most have written and received grants for their schools, and most are on numerous school committees. The administrations of the two schools rely heavily upon the talents of the four. Furthermore, in recognition of the important roles they play in their classes and schools, all have received either local or national education awards.

The four women have, within the walls of their schools, other faculty with whom to share and test ideas, plan lessons, and commiserate when necessary. At Highland Oaks, in order to implement the Coalition of Essential Schools tenet of "schools-within-a-school,"[2] Gold and Gropper belong to a team of faculty who meet regularly to discuss students and curriculum. Both told me they have at times benefited from being part of their respective teams; however, each considers the other her greatest resource within the school. Because they both teach ninth grade, the two women frequently plan units, projects, and lessons together. They brainstorm, do the necessary fieldwork (including reading works that they can potentially use in class), compare notes, and write plans together. Each woman, in separate interviews, cited the other as her greatest ally in professional life.

This strong working relationship between Gold and Gropper manifests itself in the classroom, to the benefit of all the students, because students in each class are, in effect, privy to the talents and resourcefulness of both teachers. For example, when Gropper finds an article on the difference between "love" and being "in love" to use with her students as part of a provocative introductory lesson to the study of *Romeo and Juliet*, that article is available to Gold and her students as well. Virtually every afternoon after the final bell, the two women meet to informally discuss that day's lessons. Thus they give themselves a chance to debrief, troubleshoot, assess, and, when necessary, adjust.

Teachers at Turner Tech High School also work together professionally in academy teams and/or in critical friends groups (CFGs). CFGs are groups of teachers, in Kirchner's case from the same academy and in Masztal's from several academies, who meet a few times a month (as part of teacher planning days, or during the regular school day, with substitutes provided by the administration) to talk, plan, and help each other with a wide array of educational issues. A variety of activities take place at these meetings. Teachers make presentations to their CFGs (at one CFG meeting, for example, an excellent multimedia presentation was given about ways of implementing alternative assessments); they read and discuss relevant articles (for example, members of Masztal's CFG read an article from *Educational Leadership* called "Good Seeds Grow in Strong Cultures" and then discussed how the "culture" of Turner affected things like student learning and school morale); they attend professional development programs (for example, they might learn how to use new computer software); and they sometimes break into small groups for feedback sessions on various plans or project proposals that members are working on. At one of Masztal's meetings, for example, teachers working in small groups discussed issues related to projects or units they were doing in their classes, with members of the group offering feedback. During one such session, Masztal presented one component of her "What is America?" project, wherein students were to write and present a speech with the aim of trying to answer the question, "What is America?" The speech was to be based on the evidence they had gathered from a number of sources, including, of course, the literature they had read and discussed up to that point in the semester. This written and oral presentation would count as their midterm exam. The issue at hand for Masztal was whether the evidence should in essence back up a general, intuitive claim about America, or whether the evidence should lead to a claim. As one member of the group pointed out immediately, the problem was at least partly semantic, and the group's lively discussion about what differences there might be between making a claim and then finding evidence versus gathering evidence and then making a claim helped Masztal clarify for herself exactly what she was asking of her students. At that same meeting, Masztal was of enormous help to a math teacher who was mandated by the administration to do more writing problems in math with her students. Masztal offered suggestions about framing questions as well as fashioning answers, and she also promised to provide the grateful teacher with materials about the writing process.

Effective Teachers' Influences on One Another

Whenever I observed these teachers together (for example at Dade County Council of Teachers of English meetings or at district-sponsored events), they gravitated to one another and invariably began to exchange ideas about pedagogy or specific methodologies they were using and finding effective. That is, these four women are regularly put in a position to gain new knowledge—often by district supervisors—precisely because they are the kinds of people who are hungry for new knowledge in the first place and who are willing to "go the extra mile" to make themselves the best educators they can be.

Classroom Dynamics and Intimacy

Finally, one of the most important things the four teachers have in common is that they all have a high-quality relationship with the majority of their students. Interviews with students of the teachers are full of comments about how Ms. Masztal (or Gold or Kirchner or Gropper) is "the best teacher in the school," or "the first English teacher I ever really liked," or "my role model." When asked to explain why, the students offered reasons such as these: "Well, she makes us think about things we never thought about." "You always have to go deeper with her." "It never gets boring in her class." "She chooses cool books and we have good conversations about them." "She lets you say what you feel." "She makes you work hard, but she's fair." "You really know you're learning stuff you're going to use." "She's preparing us for college." "She's preparing us for the real world." Long-term observations of the teachers with their students bears out that the teachers are liked, respected, and admired by their students.

A basic fact that contributes to classroom intimacy is that all four of these teachers love literature and love to talk about literature; they enjoy it probably more than any other component of the subject of English. It is a principal reason for their becoming English teachers in the first place. Simply put, they love "book talk" (and book talk, incidentally, plays a major role in their personal lives as well as in their professional ones [Ostrowski, 1999]). In the classroom, true literary conversations help establish a strong classroom dynamic. For fairly significant portions of their class time, they and their students are involved in conversations about literature, especially about literary characters, their actions, and the motivations for those actions. These literary conversations create a classroom dynamic that in turn creates, or at the very least verges on, intimacy.

One explanation for why this intimate classroom dynamic comes about, over time, is that each of these teachers frequently uses some form of reader-response technique to structure conversations around literary works (more on the specifics of this later). Thus, their students are not merely reading to extract information and then check with the teacher that they are "correct"; rather, they are involved in considering motives for and meanings behind characters' actions and the consequences of those actions (Rosenblatt, 1978). The primary basis for their considerations, which are encouraged and mediated by teachers and which are often expressed in heartfelt ways by students, are their own lived experiences, as well as those experiences they have lived vicariously through other texts, including films and other media with which they are familiar. The four teachers listen, sometimes affirm, sometimes ask for more information, often share their own personal experiences and reactions, and sometimes simply nod and call upon another student for further comment. Although it cannot be said to happen in every class, it often happens that these teachers create environments that allow real conversations to take place, not mere clipped exchanges between teacher and an individual student (see Nystrand, 1997). And real, heartfelt conversations are by their very nature intimate.

This sense of intimacy between teacher and class also arises out of the fact that none of the four teachers "merely" teaches English. Because Gropper and Gold each choose to teach an extra class, the prep time in their school day is insufficient for the kinds of things they both love to do with their classes. Thus, they are frequent evening and weekend visitors to the school or to one another's homes to plan, brainstorm, create. Similarly, more often than not both Kirchner and Masztal of Turner Tech can be found hours before and after the regular school day gathering materials, meeting with students to provide extra help on a project, or meeting with colleagues to plan collaborations. In the class, the fruits of this preparation, this dedication, becomes tangible. The students virtually feel it. It is contagious. Of course, this is not to say that these teachers are superhuman women who never have bad days, who never come to work less than fully prepared for every possible contingency. It is to say that they are people for whom most classes are important events—forums, if you will—where teachers' and students' minds and hearts meet for meaningful exchanges. The hour or two of class, from the start to the finish, matters. There is little wasted time. The reality of how much it matters to the teacher is readily apparent to the students, and this helps foster a classroom intimacy.

But even given that the relationships that these teachers have forged with their students are, in a particular sense, intimate, what of that? How does that affect students' learning of English? I believe it does so in several ways, including that it gives students a sense of inclusion in intellectual life, which they seem to enjoy naturally once they feel they belong. The intimate bond also fosters in students a sense of trust in their teachers, so that when teachers say, for example, that it is important to use proper subject and verb agreement in writing in order for readers to want to continue to read what a writer has to say, students readily accept that. When students receive honest C+'s on their essays, they are, quite naturally, disappointed, but they trust that the teacher does not want to falsely inflate their grades, which would only lead to greater disappointment should their first college essays, say, come back with Ds or Fs. Classroom intimacy of this kind may not be absolutely necessary for learning to take place, but I believe it enhances learning in each of these outstanding teachers' classrooms.

What Counts as English in Their Classrooms

What does it mean to be an effective teacher (or student)? As one might expect, in these four classrooms English includes the teaching and learning of certain sets of skills necessary for reading and writing (for example, the expanding of one's vocabulary, the mastering of subject-verb agreement, and the proper use of quotation marks), as well as the deepening of one's knowledge, appreciation, and understanding of literature (for example, coming to appreciate how Siddhartha's decisions can inform one's own decisions, or developing an understanding of the relationship between historical events and the literature of a period). It includes learning to articulate one's thoughts and ideas, orally as well as in writing. But the fact is that what counts as English in the four classrooms cannot be reduced to a few familiar terms, even important ones like "learning to write" or "learning about literature" or "understanding interdisciplinarity" or even "achieving high literacy." English in these classrooms involves writing, and it involves reading and talking articulately about literature and its connections to history and other disciplines; but ultimately the subject of English seems to be about possible ways of living in the world. It is about speaking with other human beings and listening to them; about trying to persuade them or understand their points of view; about collaborating with them; about communicating with them through a variety of media on a variety of topics. It is about exploring options and thinking clearly and generatively; about broadening and reflecting upon one's own perspectives; about understanding the ways in which language works; about appreciating beauty, especially the beauty that language can create; about accomplishing meaningful tasks; about nurturing creativity. Finally, in ways deeply personal and deeply public, English in these classes is about changing the world for the better.

Although ultimately the subject of English is greater than the sum of its parts, it is instructive to look at some of the components of the subject in order to see how each of the four teachers goes about presenting and teaching them to students. The following sections explore four large topics—writing, literature, mechanics and vocabulary, and oral language. Woven into these explorations are other components of English, such as test-taking skills, development of generative comprehension abilities, and strategies for learning. Where appropriate, these components are highlighted and discussed.

Teaching and Learning Writing

All four of the teachers believe that helping their students learn to write well is important. Indeed, they see writing instruction as a major part of their mission as English teachers. But the topic of writing and the teaching of writing are huge and can be approached in a variety of ways. These teachers see writing as directly and indirectly relating to reading and the study of literature, thinking and problem solving (Langer & Applebee, 1987), oral language/conversation, presenting/publishing, and creative expression. They make explicit the connections that exist between these various components. Furthermore, all of the teachers recognize and emphasize to their students that the ability to write well can empower them on several levels. It can do so on the immediate level of achieving well on large-scale tests such as the Florida Writes! Exam, as well as on important writing exercises such as college essays. Writing can also empower students on the level of personal expression, through the discovery-producing writing of personal essays, poems, and stories. The teachers are aware that the discoveries these types of writing produce involve not only personal epiphany, but also ways in which writers can create essays, poems, and stories. And finally, writing empowers students on the level of practical communication, which takes forms such as the memo, the resume, and the business letter. These practical forms are germane to many of the students' career interests.

Because writing encompasses so much—indeed, Hillocks (1995) claims that writing is at the heart of all education—the teachers must familiarize their students with the formidable variety of kinds and ways of writing. This necessitates that teachers make choices and prioritize. The kind of writing being taught and studied in the four classes depended on the specific class and the writing competence of the individuals within it, the grade level of the students, the time of year, the academy the students were part of (at Turner), the demands of the curriculum, the demands of the state, the kinds of literature they were studying, and the specific goals of a given project, unit, or lesson. The examples from the four teachers and their students represent in important ways the everyday activities in each of the classes, in all of which the amount and variety of writing done by students is enormous.

One major factor for Janas Masztal and her tenth-grade class with regard to prioritizing writing was the fact that the students would be taking the Florida Writes! Exam, a statewide test that asks students to write either persuasive or expository essays. Masztal therefore spent a significant amount of time—portions of her block-scheduled classes for a number of months prior to the test—teaching and integrating strategies for taking this particular test. Masztal was greatly aided in her efforts by workshops that had been provided by the district office in which the official Florida Writing Assessment Test Scoring Rubric was broken down and analyzed so that teachers could understand for themselves and convey to their students exactly the qualities that are found in more sophisticated writing and also would rate the highest scores. Because the Florida Writes! Exam has become an important external measure of school success in the teaching of writing in Florida, beyond the redesigned and connected curriculum, the administration of Turner Tech set aside parts of days so that all tenth-grade students in all classes practiced for the test in a variety of ways.

For example, there were several classes in which Masztal explained the rubric (a *separated* activity as discussed in Chapter 2). One follow-up writing task essentially involved the students in carefully reading and answering the question, using a given number of specific examples to back up a general thesis and using the rubric as a guide (*situated* activity). The entire class also "wrote" (via out-loud brainstorming while Masztal wrote notes, sentences, and the introductory paragraph on the blackboard) the skeleton of an essay based on a question like those asked on the Exam. Throughout the lesson, Masztal reminded students to highlight right on the page exactly what the question was asking, including whether they were to compare or contrast elements and how many examples they were to provide (situated activities). Students then wrote several mock essays on their own (simulated activity), which Masztal collected and commented upon (orally and/or in writing). Her comments focused mainly on issues of supporting claims with evidence, following a basic five-paragraph format, and developing depth and quality of ideas.

Although practicing for the Florida Writes! Exam was an important part of the curriculum for Masztal's students in the tenth grade, it was only one of many kinds of writing that her students did during the span of our study. They also wrote stories and poems. They did technical writing in the form of research reports about agriscience-related issues. And they wrote essays based on the literature they read, which often had, in some way, a relationship to agriculture (*integrated* activities).

As part of the yearlong "What is America?" project, which Masztal and the Agriscience Academy's history teacher co-organized and implemented for their common agriscience students, small groups of students put together newspapers that dealt with historical events. These were written in the present tense, as if the students were reporting an unfolding, topical event (see Ostrowski, 1999). Students also wrote book reports and literary essays on the works they read. Students told me that they liked the project a great deal for many reasons, including the following: they were learning history and English together, and knowing something about one subject helped them to better understand the other; they felt they did better on assessments in *both* subjects; and they felt they were coming to new understandings about American issues that they had never thought about or considered deeply before, such as institutionalized racism and the concept of freedom. As for Masztal herself, she particularly liked the fact that a yearlong, overarching themed project helped her organize and keep coherent her personal curriculum of having students maintain literary journals; form small groups for various discussion, research, and writing purposes; read literary and historical works; write essays, book reports, and articles; and write and give speeches.

Masztal's students kept folders containing their written work, and near the end of the year they compiled portfolios. The portfolios consisted of a variety of kinds of writing they had done over the course of that year (writings which were in every case written through several drafts), as well as paragraph-long rationales for their choices and a letter to the teacher about what "literacy" means to the student writer. Each piece in the portfolio was given a grade, and the sum of the pieces equaled the final portfolio grade. This portfolio grade was, in turn, factored into each student's overall final grade.

Because Chris Kirchner's students prepare for careers in business, they must be able to write, among other things, clear, cogent memos. "It's really important that they write memos well," Kirchner said. Early on in her teaching of the form, using her ever-present overhead projector, Kirchner demonstrated to her students the qualities of good memo writing. Before long, she had students engaged in a good deal of memo writing themselves. Kirchner then projected student memos onto the wall screen and conducted discussions with the class about the various strengths and weaknesses in their own memo writing. "Is this the absolute best way to communicate these ideas?" she would ask. "Can anyone see a way to make it even clearer?" "Is it too wordy? Can we make it more concise? Remember, it has to get the point across plainly and in as few words as possible." On most occasions ample hands were raised; Kirchner's students were almost always willing to venture their ideas. It is important to point out the process Kirchner used here: she introduced the form, practiced it, discussed it, and practiced it some more. As in the other three classrooms, learning to write is a recursive activity, involving not only writing, but listening and conversing as well.

Kirchner did not let writing end with what was merely and overtly practical for her students. They also wrote a number of major essays on subjects related to the literature they were studying. One essay, on aspects of the novel *Siddhartha*, dealt with themes that Kirchner told her eleventh-grade students would be "anchor" themes for their entire senior year and that she indeed alluded to throughout the year during their study of other literary works. These themes essentially had to do with ways of, and important decisions about, living in the world. In teams of two, the students also wrote research papers related to making civic changes in their communities. These major research papers were written over the course of several terms and included the writing and revising of proposals, as well as several drafts of the paper itself. A few of these research papers did in fact spur changes in the community. For example, the work of two young women led to the installation of a traffic light in front of Turner Tech, where early morning fender benders had been a daily occurrence. Students also wrote poems, which they worked on separately and as a whole group for several classes; this work involved students in creating poems based on unusual metaphors such as "Violence Is a New Car" and then sustaining the metaphor for a minimum of twelve lines. Kirchner spent a good deal of class time with the whole class fine-tuning these poems, from the broadest overall effects to the choices of individual words. "Is that the best word here, or is it too ordinary? I'm not sure. You tell me." Many of the poems were eventually entered in a student poetry contest. In addition to these kinds of writings, students kept stock market journals while they participated in the national "Stock Market Game" (sponsored by the Securities Industry Foundation for Economic Education), rewrote prewritten paragraphs for the purposes of recognizing and correcting typical mechanical and other stylistic errors, and wrote sentences and paragraphs for various homework assignments, often in answer to questions related to the literature they were reading.

Probably the most important tool in Kirchner's repertoire of methodologies for teaching her students to write formal essays comes from Toulmin (1958), who instructs that well-argued essays follow a pattern of *claim*, *data*, and *warrant*. She doesn't so much expect her students to become experts in the Toulmin category sets as habitual users of its essential components. Kirchner knows that students find Toulmin's method difficult, but she believes that when they do come to understand it, over time, it helps them organize their thinking and writing effectively. In preparing her students to write essays, Kirchner constantly reminded them that not only were they making a claim, but also they must warrant their data if their essay was to be fully convincing. "If it's from the text, it's data," she told them. She provided them with strategies: "If you have trouble warranting, write a sentence that begins with 'if.'" She made explicit certain kinds of learning they would achieve: "Focus on warranting will lead you to the analytical thinking that so many people are claiming students in the twenty-first century will need." After assessing papers (with comments like "this must be explained, step by step" and "explained thinking is what's called a *warrant*"), Kirchner reviewed the essays with the students on the overhead projector and pointed out, among other things, the strengths and weaknesses of the papers based on their claims, data, and warrants. She showed the students a paper that was at the rough draft stage and then another that was much more fully developed, and compared the two. "You see how much more developed this writer's warrant is?" All the while, the students had their own papers in front of them so that they could compare what they had done with the two works projected on the wall.

Like Masztal, Kirchner had students select and edit pieces of writing they had done over the course of each year for their portfolios. Portfolios were assessed holistically and factored into students' overall grades.

In addition to all the other kinds of writing they did, both Masztal's and Kirchner's students (in fact, all students at Turner) produced and revised resumes, the writing and shaping of which took place mainly in English classes, where the teachers used professional resumes as models appropriate to the students' own vocations. In producing resumes, students were trained to recall all relevant experiences and were taught how best to represent those experiences in order to attract the attention of potential employers and/or educators.

Like students in Masztal's and Kirchner's classes, Rita Gold's and Susan Gropper's students were constantly writing *something*. One of the writing tasks Gold's students worked very hard on, which required and developed critical thinking skills, was an essay comparing and contrasting Thurber's short story "The Secret Life of Walter Mitty" with the film version. Before viewing the film, the students had read the story and spent several classes discussing it, both in whole-group conversations with the teacher and, at times, in their literature circles (literature circles are discussed in more detail below). After viewing the film, Gold and her students engaged in an in-class, whole-group discussion in which students read separate short essays about the different styles of two current-day comedians. Using a series of Venn diagrams on the board, Gold had students come to the board to fill in either the separate or overlapping Venn diagrams depending upon whether the point they were making was one the two comedians had in common or not. Thus, only after reading, discussing, viewing, and brainstorming together about comedic styles did the students write individual essays comparing and contrasting the written and the film versions of the Walter Mitty story. By the time they actually wrote their essays, they had not only become well prepared to write a comparison/contrast essay, but they'd also become much more media-savvy as a result of knowing the written story well and then seeing and talking about the liberties the filmmakers took with it, either by necessity or for their own purposes. They had also gained strategies they could apply to future writing. Thus, on the way to further developing their literacy skills as writers, they also grew as thinkers and oral language users, and, particularly important in the current day, they became more media-literate as well.

In addition to their writing a number of formal essays like the one described above, Gold's students also engaged in less formal writings. For example, in conjunction with the literature they read, especially with longer works like Zindel's *The Pigman*, they kept response logs. In these logs, students sometimes were asked to write reflections on specific questions related to the work. For example, Gold asked the students to choose a sentence from a particular chapter of the novel and explain in a paragraph or two why they liked that sentence. At another time, she asked them to choose a sentence from a particular chapter that they did not like. At still other times, students were free to respond to the work, or parts of it, in any way they pleased. These response logs connected the activities of reading and writing. Students saw and discovered what they thought in the process of reflecting for the purpose of writing. The activity of isolating and commenting on individual sentences, for example, helped students see the relationship between a part and the whole. When a student chose a sentence that could be said to contain the crux of the entire work's meaning, Gold was ready to make that knowledge overt for the whole class (e.g., "The sentence Jermel chose is very important, because, as he says . . ."). This kind of writing exercise also helped students to better understand the craft that goes into writing good sentences, especially when elements of the sentence were pointed out and made explicit. Finally, response logs reinforced—as did so many of the writing assignments in the class—the *habit* of writing, which for these students and their teacher was a natural and important part of what "English" is.

One of the interesting formal writing projects Susan Gropper's students undertook also involved writing about *The Pigman*. After reading the book (at times together in class, and at times individually, either in class or at home) and discussing it (at times as a whole group and at other times in literature circles), the students wrote essays in which they selected one of the two central teenage protagonists, John or Lorraine, and explained why they would like that character for a friend. Like most writing assignments given by the four teachers, the writing of this paper developed over time and involved strategies that could be used for other writing. First, with the aid of graphic organizers, which give students visual and verbal clues about organizing their materials into related sections (sometimes rough clusters, sometimes paragraphs), the students got their basic ideas down on paper so that they could examine them, alter them, and/or develop them. Second, they wrote a first draft, or "sloppy copy." Then they met in small groups to give one another feedback on these drafts. Last (almost last) they wrote final, edited drafts that they were permitted to show to another classmate for final inspection before handing the paper in.

Near the end of the year, the students in both Gold's and Gropper's classes selected several pieces from the many writings they had done over the course of that year to add to their portfolios. They were given time to rewrite one final time before adding materials to the portfolio, which would follow them to their next grade level. In the case of Gold's and Gropper's students, that meant that their portfolios would go to the appropriate teachers at the high school they would be attending in the fall.

Clearly, the students of these four effective teachers have been shown the importance of writing in their current lives as well as in their future lives. They have been involved in many kinds of writing experiences. They have written with different audiences in mind and for different purposes. They write so regularly that writing is a habit. They also know that writing is an act of discovery, and that the aims of most kinds of writing are rarely accomplished in a single draft. They have been made conscious of the connections between writing and reading, writing and talking, and writing and other media. It is natural for these student writers to think of writing as a process that involves some solo work but also a good deal of collaboration.

In interviews, some of the students said that they had come to enjoy writing. The enjoyment has come as a result of their writing experiences in the class of one of these teachers. A number of students expressed a confidence in themselves as writers that they claimed they did not have before. One young woman, for example, in reflecting upon the experience of writing a long-term research paper in Masztal's class, wrote, "I know I can write a good research paper now."

There are several discernable reasons for these students' growing confidence as writers. For one thing, writing was clearly characterized for them as an important part of life itself, not just one of the things done in English class. In one way or another, all of the teachers made it clear to their students that their ability to write would have profound and practical effects on the quality of their lives, whether it be in affecting their ability to go to the college of their choice, or in expressing themselves in ways necessary to get and hold jobs. Teachers referred to their own experiences as student writers a number of times. Teachers often brought up these things as a way of explaining to the students why they were doing whatever given kind of writing activities they were doing at the time. They also mentioned them in explaining the importance of getting feedback and of writing multiple drafts.

Even students who simply did not like to write (several were inter-viewed) understood that they needed to write at least competently or they wouldn't reach their goals in life.

Teachers made it clear that writing well meant writing often—and all of their students wrote often, virtually every day, in fact—for example, in journals or to answer discussion questions or in drafting "major" essays. Writing well also meant soliciting as much useful feed-back from others as possible, which the teachers facilitated by forming small "writing groups" (Elbow, 1973). Writing well meant that a good deal of revising would be involved in most kinds of writing. As stu-dents internalized the elements that went into good writing, it became more and more natural for them to think of writing as a process and an act of discovery. They were less resistant to the recursive and looping process of brainstorming, drafting, discussing, revising, and editing that is usually involved in writing well. Students not only did a lot of writing but also understood why they were doing it. And the more writing they did, the more comfortable and confident they felt doing it.

Teaching and Learning Mechanics and Vocabulary

For the four teachers profiled here, teaching writing and teaching mechanics, if not vocabulary, are virtually inseparable parts of the same whole. Nevertheless, all of the teachers devote some class time to the specific teaching of mechanics and vocabulary. One, Chris Kirch-ner, dedicated significantly more time to these things than the other three. In fact, Kirchner calls herself the "grammar queen." She believes that if her traditionally disadvantaged students are to succeed in the world of business, they will need well-developed writing and speak-ing skills, and so she dedicates a fair portion of class time to the teach-ing of mechanics. Though Kirchner can talk "street" as well as any teacher, and sometimes does so with her students, she believes, and tells her students quite often, that street language, either spoken or written, will not enable them to succeed either in college or in the busi-ness world. Based on interviews, the students have come to agree "If you write something like that in college, they'll laugh at you." Because the students are motivated to get into college and/or have successful careers (and at least part of that general motivation can be attributed to the academy structure at Turner—see Ostrowski, 1999), they tend to pay attention when Kirchner teaches grammar. She has convinced them that it matters. As one of Kirchner's students put it, "If you hand in a paper in college and it's all misspelled and the grammar's all messed up, they won't take you seriously. They might not even read what you wrote."

So how does Kirchner teach grammar? She does it both in an integrated fashion within the context of the students' own writing as well as through separated and situated grammar lessons. During one class, Kirchner spent an hour or so of her two-hour block in teaching students about compound sentences, complex sentences, and compound-complex sentences. The students were not only engaged, they appeared to have a great time. Rather than lecturing about these kinds of sentences and the differences between them, Kirchner had student volunteers come to the front of the classroom and actually become grammatical parts of sentences. She did this by taping large plastic signs onto their chests that read "coordinating conjunction" and "dependent clause." "Oooo, Ms. Kirchner, Ms. Kirchner," one enthusiastic young man called out, straining his arm toward her from his desk. "I want to be an independent clause. Pleeeeeeeease." And an independent clause he became. When all the necessary sentence "parts" were gathered in front of the room, Kirchner began to ask the class where, for example, Keisha, who was a prepositional phrase, belonged in a complex sentence. "Put her right up there at the front, Ms. Kirchner," a young man said. "Then you need Bertrand next to her." "Is he right about that?" Ms. Kirchner asked the class. "Yep," they responded.

When asked about the always thorny issue of whether this kind of exercise actually carries over into their writing, Kirchner asserted that the exercise was not done merely for the fun of it, nor even merely for the purpose of engaging the students. Rather, she believed that because she constantly stresses the importance of the relationship between the mechanics of writing and overtly helps students make connections to actual good writing—and because she uses enjoyable and unusual methods—students do learn the grammar, and that learning does contribute to improvement in their overall writing skills. "They do become better writers," says Kirchner.

Kirchner constantly reinforced the mechanics she had already taught in isolation when, for example, she went over student papers on the overhead projector. If, in going over a student paper with the class, she saw a place where two or three simple sentences could have been combined, she would ask the class if there was any other way the writer could have presented the same information in order to create more sentence variety. "She could put those two sentences into one," a student might suggest. "Good, and what do we call that?" "Complex? No. Compound? Yeah, compound." "You got it!"

Thus, teaching grammar is part of the conversation that is English in Kirchner's class. Even the learning of certain rules of grammar is an active endeavor in this class. Furthermore, Kirchner makes sure the reasons are overt for students' knowing grammar and using what they know.

While none of the other three teachers seems to enjoy the teaching of grammar to the extent that Kirchner does, they all recognize that for most of their students, writing well necessitates both some isolated learning of skills and a lot of practice at using skills in the context of whatever writing they are doing at the time. For example, for a time, Masztal dedicated a part of every Friday's class to topics such as subject-verb agreement and the uses of subordinate clauses. She would lecture a bit about the properties of the given item of study, give examples on the board, and then have students practice the skill, sometimes using prepared worksheets. She would emphasize that in the next piece of graded essay writing they did, she would be grading for content as well as for the particular skill or skills being studied. In this way, Masztal connected the isolated study of a particular skill with the contextualized, larger, and generally more meaningful writing the students were doing.

Rather than dedicating long parts of a class to mechanics, Gropper preferred to teach grammar in five- to ten-minute minilessons near the beginning of some classes. For example, upon entering the class, students were directed to look at the side board, which asked them, in one case, to copy five sentences written on the board and insert the necessary quotation marks in the proper places. Gropper then invited five volunteers to come to the board, add the quotation marks, and explain why they put them where they did, as well as what purpose they serve in the sentence. Later, as the class read and discussed a part of a short story, Gropper interrupted a literary thought to say, "Notice the quotation marks around the character's actual words." Gropper, like all of the effective teachers in this study, was conscious of reinforcing and integrating what students learned in one domain or context in other domains or contexts when the opportunity presented itself. These four teachers are all natural "connectors," because they recognize that ultimately the various elements of English form a whole, and because they know that for learning to take place they must model these connections for students and reinforce them as often as they can.

All four teachers interwove vocabulary with the study of literature and the act of writing. If a new word related to the study of mechanics, or technology, or pertained to a specific academy at the school (e.g., "divest" in the business academy) the teacher would define and explain it, as necessary. In all four cases, most vocabulary words came directly from the stories, poems, plays, novels, articles, and essays the students were reading. Sometimes, in going through a piece, important new words were pointed out by the teacher, and the class highlighted them before the piece was read. Then, during the reading of the piece, the class would discuss a new word's meaning based on contextual clues and structural analysis. Sometimes, certain words were selected by the teacher and discussed before students read a piece, so that when they encountered the words in the piece, they would have some initial familiarity with them and could see them used in the specific context of that work. Gropper sometimes assigned homework in which students were to draw pictures or illustrations that depicted the meanings of the vocabulary words they were studying—which, again, came from some context (usually literary) relevant to their other work in English. Many of Gropper's students displayed a good deal of artistic talent in completing these assignments. As with most of the separate components, there were deliberate attempts by the teachers to contextualize vocabulary, connect it, and make it relevant to a larger vision of what English is.

For all four teachers, assessing mechanics was occasionally done via specific grammar quizzes and tests (Kirchner, for example, had students rewrite paragraphs that she had written with deliberate mechanical errors), but more commonly assessment was factored into their writing assignments. With formal essays, the teachers most often gave multiple grades, specifying components like content, support (evidence, warrant), organization (form), style, and, of course, mechanics.

Teaching and Learning Literature

Before describing some of the ways literature is taught in the four teachers' classrooms, I want to mention some of the works the teachers chose to use (in each case, the teachers did in fact choose the works; they were not mandated). These included many of those found on lists of typical literary works dealt with in high school classes (Applebee, 1993), including works of Shakespeare, Fitzgerald, Whitman, and Thurber. The four teachers also taught works that might be said to be achieving modern canonical status, works like *The Pigman*, *A Day No Pigs Would Die*, *Their Eyes Were Watching God*, *I Know Why the Caged Bird Sings*, and *Bless Me, Ultima*. Other works studied included contemporary novels like *The Color of Water* and Paulsen's *The Car*, as well as numerous short stories and poems.

It is rare that any of the four teachers speaks for more than a few minutes in class before involving students in at least some discussion.

Students' voices frequently dominated structured yet freewheeling conversations around literary works, with very little input from the teacher for long stretches of time (this was most pronounced in Kirchner's class).

The following paragraphs describe one such occasion, or "event,"—a Socratic Seminar on the topic of Herman Hesse's *Siddhartha*, held in Kirchner's senior class. It took place in the month of October during the second year of the study.

For Kirchner, the idea of the Socratic Seminar comes out of a "toolbox" of ideas from the Coalition of Essential Schools; the aim is for *all* students, not just those deemed academically superior, to be given a forum in which demonstrate their knowledge and express their ideas. Kirchner has participated with other faculty in training sessions for conducting Socratic Seminars. Her comfort level with them, she says, increases each time she conducts one.

In the view of many educators, one of the hallmarks of a good teacher (and a good thinker in general) is her or his ability to tailor an idea to a specific situation so as to maximize the idea's relevance and effectiveness in that situation. Kirchner is nothing if not an expert educational "tailor." As she conducts them, Socratic Seminars are special events that involve a good deal of preparation and scaffolding on her part and on the parts of her students. For example, students did not merely read the work and then come in on the designated day and sit facing each other and begin talking about what they liked and didn't like about the book. Instead, by the time the Socratic Seminar on *Siddhartha* took place, students had all (1) read the book and participated in class discussions about some aspects of it (other aspects, by Kirchner's design, would come up for the first time during the seminar); (2) been given, in groups of four or five students, a specific question that dealt with a particular and important aspect of the book, and that involved either some research or some in-depth analysis (for example, describing the basic tenets of Hinduism, or analyzing the symbolic meaning[s] of rivers in the novel); and (3) written, individually and independently, a major essay on some aspect of the small group's question, due on the morning of the seminar. For her part, Kirchner had created an "essential question" for the entire unit on *Siddhartha*: "What suggestions for living in the modern world are offered in *Siddhartha*?" She had also carefully prepared about ten larger student questions (i.e., questions that dealt with even more thought-provoking and crosscutting issues than their small-group work had), read and commented on early drafts of student papers, sat in on small groups as they worked out their responses to their questions, prepared the class for the procedure of a Socratic Seminar, and informed them about the criteria by which they would be evaluated. These criteria included: (1) students' demeanor and decorum during the seminar (both of which she had carefully explained); (2) their background knowledge of the author and the work; (3) the quality of their claims, data, and warrants; and (4) their ability to connect to others' points. Kirchner also created and printed out copies of a rubric that she invited guests—generally other faculty and staff at Turner—to fill out during or after observing the seminar. Finally, Kirchner invited students from the Broadcasting Academy to film the seminar so that her students could view it later and analyze the conversation.

On the day of the *Siddhartha* seminar, Kirchner arranged the desks into two large sections that faced each other. After a discussion about the students' experiences in writing their papers on *Siddhartha*, which they had handed in that morning, the seminar itself began. Kirchner asked one of the small groups to present its findings about Hinduism. Each member of the group reported on a different aspect of the religion. The reports were punctuated with personal comments such as, "This part really surprised me . . ." and "This is a lot like my own religion . . ." When students not in the reporting group raised their hands, either Kirchner or the student who was currently speaking called on them, and they contributed further information, asked questions, or made personal comments. It went this way with all the groups, whose topics ranged from the just-described factual type to the much more analytical type, involving for example, the way the author treats the question of sexuality. The following transcript excerpt is offered to suggest the flavor of the conversation that took place that day. Note how seamlessly the students relate aspects of the novel to their own lives and situations, and how they build conversation by commenting upon or alluding to one another's comments.

Joe: The concept that was brought out about Siddhartha and Bovinda was that Bovinda was a seeker, and that because of him seeking her, he wanted to obtain the highest position, he missed a lot of other things, and Siddhartha being not a seeker, saw and got to experience. So tie in with Jennifer and everyone else's comments, I just wanted to throw that in.

Kirchner: Gina.

Gina: This is our time, in our particular situation being in business. Siddhartha would be like the entrepreneur, the person that definitely goes out to be what they want; they wanted their own laws, they want to learn their own way, they want to be [inaudible]. Bovinda would be the person that would be content, have somebody to tell you that yes, this is right, this is wrong, the person who would go to a major corporation and fill in a position there, and have the security of being in a major corporation.

Joe: I'm glad that Gina brought that point up about the analysis for today. Because I completely forgot that until she mentioned it. I find that to bring it down to our level, I know many of us are planning on going to school with our friends, you know, are going away to college to party with our friends, because we don't want to go alone on the road of life. So, many of us are going to give up the accomplishments that we might have been able to attain for that friendship. . . . I just . . . never really looked at that before. I know with me personally, I didn't want to go away to college, because I didn't want to be away from friends and family. And sometimes, in order to get what you need to get done, you need to go it alone.

The entire seminar was characterized by such talk: students spoke with knowledge of the novel and with a good deal of passion. They listened respectfully to one another, and even when they disagreed with one another, they did so in a manner that was careful to warrant their own claims; and they did so with the utmost respect for one another's opinions and beliefs.

Kirchner's students were able to enjoy such a "grand conversation" because in essence they had been learning to participate in such conversations for a long time, certainly since they'd entered her class. (I observed many occasions where such conversations took place around literature or related topics.) In these conversations, the students' ideas and opinions were not only tolerated or even respected by Kirchner, but also actively solicited; students' voices "counted" so long as what they said could be "backed up," or warranted with data. When students related stories of personal experience, these stories were listened to respectfully and often commented upon by Kirchner and other students. Furthermore, Kirchner regularly shared her personal experiences with the class, often relating them to the works the class was studying or to topics they were discussing. Thus, she modeled for her students various forms that reader's responses and good literary conversations could take.

For all four of the teachers, the study of literature can be looked at as a kind of invitation to enter a literary world. One of the ways

Susan Gropper invited her students into the study of literary works was through the use of prediction. This method exploits and makes conscious what already happens on a subconscious level in the minds of readers; that is, readers are always making predictions about what will come next, based on a number of factors, including the title of the work or a chapter title, what has already happened in the work, what has happened in other works that might be relevant, and what has happened to readers in their real lives or in lives they know about. Pleasure and surprise in reading can be derived both from having expectations met (predictions confirmed) and from having them thwarted.

Gropper began the study and discussion of several works of literature, including "The Secret Life of Walter Mitty," by asking her students to write a brief prediction of what the story would be about based solely on the title. After allowing them to think and write for a few minutes, Gropper asked for volunteers to read or tell what they'd written. Student responses revealed a fairly wide range of predictions, and in each case Gropper was careful to ask the student to articulate the relationship between the title and his or her prediction. In that way, even in this fairly informal context, students had to defend their responses with careful thinking and reasoning. The students then went on to read the first paragraph and write another prediction about what the story was about, which again was discussed. Finally they read the entire first page, and then followed the same procedure of writing a prediction and then discussing it. By the time they were ready to discontinue making formal predictions about the story, the students appeared keen to discover whether or not their predictions would be accurate. That is, they were motivated to read. Thus, in the course of twenty or twenty-five minutes, Gropper had them reading, writing, and talking about "The Secret Life of Walter Mitty."

Another way of inviting students into the literature they are reading is the use of literature circles, small groups within the larger group which are brought together for various purposes relating to the study of a work of literature. The teachers described in this chapter use small groups frequently, and they cited many reasons for doing so. For example, students who are reluctant speakers in large groups are often effusive in small groups; thus they are able to practice public speaking in a nonthreatening environment. Also, small groups encourage turn taking and collaborative and generative thinking. Ideas contributed by one member build upon or challenge the ideas of other members. Students are exposed to multiple perspectives on literary issues, including perspectives that they may not have anticipated and that alter their thinking in profound ways. Finally, in small groups like literature circles, students play various roles and thus learn various ways in which one can function in a group.

Gold is a great believer in literature circles, for all of the above-mentioned reasons. In her literature circles, students are assigned roles as "leader" (leads the discussion), "page" (takes notes or keeps minutes), "reporter" (gives oral report of group's discussion to the larger group), and "taskmaster" (makes sure the group stays on task). In one of Gold's classes, literature circles met to discuss aspects of *The Pigman*. Students were asked to create a diagram of the novel's plot, to identify the central conflict in the novel, to identify a major theme of the novel, and to describe each of the central characters. Most of the groups were quite lively, and students seemed to take their roles seriously. (Roles changed often throughout the year so that each student in a group played each role at one time or another.) A few of the groups seemed quiet and hesitant to get under way, or perhaps uncertain of how to proceed. These were the groups where Gold spent the majority of her time, injecting a good deal of energy and guidance.

A related method that Gold (and Gropper) occasionally employed was that of "jigsawing." There were times during the semester when Gold gave each literature circle a choice of seven or eight books to read. In one case, this was done in conjunction with a multicultural research report students were expected to write, with each of the seven or eight books addressing a cultural topic or being written by a member of a given culture or ethnicity. After agreeing on a book within the circle, each member of the literature circle read the book, and as a group they discussed it and wrote about it. Jigsawing called for one member of each literature circle to move into a different literature circle and discuss with the new group the book that his or her group had read. In this way, all the groups got to hear about the books their group had not chosen to read. The member who described the book to the new group was referred to by Gold as the "expert" on that book, a label students took a great deal of pride in having. Gold reported that as a result of the jigsawing technique, many students asked if they could read the book an expert had described to them.

What about the study of poetry? Some teachers and students complain that the study of poetry is, for a variety of reasons, difficult. Even students who enjoy writing poetry can resist studying the poetry of others. One engaging poetry lesson took place at Turner Tech in Janas Masztal's class. The poem under consideration was Whitman's "I Hear America Singing"—an apt selection given that this was the year of Masztal's "What is America?" project. The especially interesting and fun part of this lesson involved Masztal's assigning each group of five or six students to give a choral reading of the poem to the rest of the class. After first reading a few paragraphs in a textbook that gave some necessary background information about Whitman, and then having the class read and discuss the poem as a whole group, Masztal sent the various small groups off to their own meeting places around the Agriscience Academy's minicampus to prepare a choral reading, or performance, of the poem. The students were instructed to be as creative and as personally interpretive as they could. One group went out to the gazebo beside the canal, where they worked out a routine: a different student read each verse in the voice of a particular character while the others provided background sound appropriate to that character's livelihood (for example, the sound of a saw for a carpenter and the sound of a wailing baby for a mother.) The preparation for the presentation unfolded just as Masztal would have liked, a blend of fun and seriousness that kept the students on-task but with frequent injections of humor and wit on their part. For the final fifteen minutes of class, groups presented their choral readings, to the great enjoyment of all.

What did Masztal accomplish by "teaching" the poem in this way and not in a more traditional fashion? First of all, on the macro level, by teaching the poem in the context of the larger, yearlong theme of "What is America?" she enabled the students to immediately anchor the individual work to that theme, about which they had already been thinking, talking, and writing a great deal. Having this anchor gave them a chance to think critically about how the characters Whitman describes and the issues the poem implicitly raises related to their evolving sense of what America is.

On a more micro level, she enabled the students to take the poem off the page and put it into their own throats. In order to work out an effective choral reading that wouldn't embarrass them in front of their classmates, students had to talk about the poem with each other. They had to negotiate and voice opinions: "No, that's not the way he'd sound, I think he'd have a deeper voice. And maybe out of breath." It is fair to say that as a result of learning the poem this way, many of the students will remember "I Hear America Singing" for a long time.

Like all the teachers in this study, Masztal explored a variety of literary genres with her students. In addition to poetry, they read novels, short stories, and essays. During the year of the "What is America?" project, all the readings were somehow related to that overarching question. Students discussed these literary, journalistic, and historical works in their small groups and as a whole group, and, like the students of the other teachers discussed in this chapter, regularly wrote in conjunction with their reading and their conversations around that reading. Even after doing their daily sustained silent reading, students wrote for five minutes in their journals about whatever they'd been reading, including feelings and thoughts based on that reading. In all these ways, students were making connections between thinking, reading, and writing; and thinking, reading, and writing were more and more becoming habitual for the students.

Of course, the study of literature for the four teachers is, on the most fundamental plane, about "reading." And students must first and foremost do the reading, which is in itself a challenge confronting many English/language arts teachers. One comes away with a strong sense that the majority of the students in these classes are reading. Given that, the study of literature becomes an invitation to an in-depth conversation about what one has read, not only for the purpose of knowing what a given piece of literature is "about," but also for the way a given piece of literature can reveal insights about life and about oneself. It is the kind of envisionment building that Langer describes (1995). It is about exchanging thoughts and contributing ideas and perspectives as part of a larger conversation where these ideas and perspectives mingle and mix and affect each other in unpredictable ways. The topics are varied, from issues of history and culture to the myriad personal motives that drive human actions. For many students, including those who may be silenced in various ways by school culture, the study of literature is about gaining confidence in one's own voice. It is about moving deeper into the knowledge of the ways language conveys meanings. These are valuable experiences and valuable tools for anyone who will ever be asked to think through a problem, interpret a situation, investigate a motive, or use language for any of a thousand purposes in any of a thousand situations.

It should be noted here again that the study of literature in these four classrooms is not isolated from other components of English but is instead intricately related to them. Much of the reading the students do is accompanied by or followed up with writing, just as it is accompanied by or followed up with conversation. Furthermore, teachers make these connections explicit, so that students form the general habit of looking for the relationships between things and trust that the search will yield interesting results. Finally, in speaking of habits, it must be mentioned that many of the students interviewed and observed for this study have become habitual readers as a result of their experiences in their English classes, due in large part to their coming to accept their teachers' invitations to explore literary works.

English and the Uses of Oral Language

In describing just a few of the many activities that comprise English in the classrooms of these four teachers, I have already touched upon the uses of oral language in their classrooms, because oral language is essential to virtually every one of those activities. The purpose for this brief section is to isolate "oral language" from contexts and examples already given for the purpose of analyzing the role it plays and the contributions it makes to students' learning.

Whether in a career-oriented environment like that of Turner Tech or a more academically oriented one like Highland Oaks, one of the first benefits for students who are given many opportunities to present their thoughts and ideas orally is that it is excellent preparation for many careers in which it is necessary to be comfortable presenting information and ideas to other people. Literary conversations like the ones that take place regularly in the four teachers' classes, for example, helped students feel comfortable and confident about expressing themselves in front of others. In many cases they were thinking "on their feet," articulating ideas that were only then, in the midst of the activity, forming and re-forming as students interacted with texts, teachers, and one another.

The students were being trained, furthermore, to be able to defend their ideas not only in writing but also in speaking, whether it be as a result of Kirchner's insistence on their always "warranting their data," or of presenting solid, defendable "evidence," as Masztal put it for her students in the "What is America?" midterm speech. Gold often asked multiple whys of her students when she felt their oral responses to her or other students' inquiries were inadequately developed or defended. Nor was Gropper one to allow a brief oral response to substitute for a more developed one. "Tell me more about that," was a frequent comment. These teachers were developing in their students an understanding of the need to articulate one's thoughts as fully and thoughtfully as possible.

All four of the teachers saw the study of English as a kind of grand conversation in which as many voices and as many perspectives as possible were invited in. The intimate atmosphere, the acceptance of many viewpoints so long as they were informed in some way, the literary works themselves that were so full of ideas ripe for conversation, and the teachers' passion for "book talk"—all these things contributed to environments in which oral language played a key role in learning.

Finally, all four teachers used small groups for the purposes of research, writing, and the study of literature. In these groups, even reluctant, shy students often felt comfortable enough to lend their voices to conversations. Students in small groups learned to listen to one another, to negotiate the best ways to make their voices heard in the group, and to be open to changing their perspectives based on the voiced perspectives of others.

Taking Stock

All four of the teachers profiled in this chapter are unusual in their dedication to their students, their involvement in education on many levels, their creativity as teachers, and their hunger as learners and innovators. Even after a relatively brief examination of their class-rooms, it is fair to say that English in these classrooms encompasses a wide and varied, but interrelated, range of educational terrains. The four teachers see it as their mandate to provide a rich array of literacy-related activities and experiences for their students—activities and experiences that revolve around wide reading, wide writing, expansive and prolonged thinking and problem solving, and ample opportunities for conversing about and presenting what they are learning to faculty as well as to one another—so that they can make intelligent, informed decisions in personal and public matters throughout their lives. The teachers are preparing the students not only to be flexible in their abilities to find and use knowledge and information, and to make connections between many pockets of knowledge, but also to create new knowledge.

Furthermore, the students are learning to understand them-selves and other human beings and the needs and desires and capabili-ties that make them human. While practical matters such as getting into college and getting good jobs are often emphasized as motivators in these classrooms, none of the teachers has lost sight of the important aesthetic value in activities such as studying and discussing literature and writing creatively. Students come away from these classrooms pre-pared for what comes next, be it another year of high school or the transition to college or a job, but they also come away more reflective about what's already come in their lives, and what all of it might mean.

5 An Effective Teacher in a Newcomers' School

Ester Helmar-Salasoo
The National Research Center on English Learning & Achievement

with

Sally Jo Bronner
Institute for Cultural Partnerships

Paola R. Bonissone
University at Albany, State University of New York

*T*he increase in the numbers of students of cultural and linguistic diversity has placed tremendous organizational demands on schools and new pedagogical demands on teachers. The persistently high failure rate of U.S. schools to adequately educate English Language Learners is well documented in statistics of high school dropout rates and low literacy levels. Inner-city schools in particular enroll many—sometimes a majority of—students who speak a language other than English. Schools often look for more effective solutions than those they are currently using.

The traditional ways of teaching ESOL (English for Speakers of Other Languages) usually don't include much reading, writing, talking, or thinking, based on the belief that the students must first learn the English language, mostly taught through oral language and short text exercises. Often, the linguistic and cultural resources of students are excluded in order to focus on learning English language skills and uses. Such students are often isolated from native English students in separate ESOL classes where they work from ESOL texts. Yet, an environment where students have little opportunity to talk, read substantive texts, think, and write at length can restrict their opportunity to use what they already know to gain both language development and higher literacy. This chapter focuses on a school that takes quite a different approach to English language learning.

Marsha Slater teaches language arts at International High School, an alternative high school for students who have lived in the United States less than four years and have scored lower than the 21st percentile on the English Language Assessment Battery Test. In 1997–98, International enrolled 451 students from forty-eight countries speaking thirty-seven languages. The school is extraordinary in every aspect—from its democratic leadership, to its language-rich interdisciplinary academic programs, to its collegial and supportive environment, to its high graduation and college acceptance rates.

Slater's classroom is a rich literacy community. If it were filled with native English speakers, it would be viewed as excellent. But given the varied language background of Slater's students, what occurs in her classroom is a remarkable achievement because it shows how English language learners can develop high literacy if someone trusts them enough.

This chapter begins by describing the school. It then discusses the professional environments in which Slater works and in which she has participated throughout her teaching career, as well as the specific ways in which she helps her students become highly literate language users. The chapter illustrates the connectedness between professional influences, teacher approaches, and student achievement.

The School

International High School is nestled near "America's most diverse neighborhood" (Page, 1997). This multicultural neighborhood serves as a stepping-stone onto American soil. It welcomes newcomers with an array of familiar ethnic stores, restaurants, and faces. Most immigrants are likely to find somebody in these surrounds who has made the long trek from the same native country.

The school is housed at LaGuardia Community College in a busy nonresidential area. It is near one of the major traffic bridges to Manhattan and has several noisy roads nearby. A major form of transportation to the school is train, and many students commute long distances to attend. The train snakes past the school on an elevated track, leaving an ugly metal scar in its wake. The neighborhood is run-down and splashed with graffiti, but there are also a few newly painted and restored large buildings and warehouses. There are no residential homes around the school. Instead, a correctional facility stands diagonally opposite the college, and a factory hides in the next block. The odd bagel and coffee cart sits out on the gum-plastered sidewalk, feeding the constant stream of students.

LaGuardia Community College welcomes its students with a huge banner. Once inside, International High School students need to make their way past security guards, down hallways, and past the college library, to the basement where the high school is housed. The busy office, staffed by students, is the first stop at the high school. The nearby hallway is decked with displays, such as two bold notice boards with information about the Chinese Club and about Ecuador. Other notice boards proudly list the universities, public and private, to which members of last year's graduating class were accepted (including Columbia, MIT, Cornell, the University of Chicago, and many others).

Program Structure

The school's instructional offerings are grouped into six thematically based interdisciplinary programs. Students are assigned to a cluster for the year. Within each cluster, students study humanities and math/science/technology with the group of teachers assigned to that cluster. Each cluster studies two themes (one for each semester), such as "Motion," "Visibility/Invisibility," and "American Dream." The school runs seventy-minute periods six times a day from 8 A.M. to 3:25 P.M. Each teaching team is responsible for creating its own curriculum, scheduling classes, and determining assessment procedures. International High School relies primarily on portfolios for assessment. Students' portfolios, successful course completion, and receiving the minimum number of course credits form the basis of high school graduation. By the time students graduate, most will usually have made use of LaGuardia's two-year-college facilities and courses. They will also have completed two required internships of about thirteen weeks each (a minimum of four days a week) conducted either on campus or in the community.

Educational Philosophy

The community of the school has evolved through vigilant adherence and commitment to the school's mission statement, which outlines its goals and principles. It is worth repeating here:

1. Limited-English-proficiency (LEP) students require the ability to understand, speak, read, and write English with near-native fluency to realize their full potential within an English-speaking society.

2. In an increasingly interdependent world, fluency in a language other than English must not be viewed as a handicap,

but rather as a resource for the student, the school, and the society.

3. Language skills are most effectively learned in context and emerge most naturally in purposeful, language-rich, interdisciplinary study.

4. The most successful educational programs are those which emphasize high expectations coupled with effective support systems.

5. Individuals learn best from each other in heterogeneous, collaborative groupings.

6. The carefully planned use of multiple learning contexts in addition to the classroom (e.g., learning centers, career internship sites, field trips) facilitates language acquisition and content-area mastery.

7. Career education is a significant motivational factor for adolescent learners.

8. The most effective instruction takes place when teachers actively participate in the school's decision-making process, including instructional program design, curriculum development, and materials selection.

Interdisciplinary Study

In International's interdisciplinary approach, the curriculum of the entire school is linked thematically. Students are required to make connections between the disciplines. For example, one cluster of students studies the overarching theme "Motion" over the whole first semester (about twenty weeks), and the more specific topic "Forces" over a period of four weeks in all of the subject areas: humanities (language arts, social studies, and art) and math/science/technology. Teacher-created "activity guides," rather than textbooks or workbooks, form the curricular and instructional framework. Students respond to literature and work together through projects in small groups via these activity guides. (See Appendix D for a sample activity guide.) Students not only develop a broad and deep repertoire of language skills but also write a mastery essay in which they synthesize their knowledge and critical thinking skills within and across the content areas.

The teamwork necessary to create, revise, and teach these interdisciplinary programs requires teachers to model collaborative work to their students, who then engage in collaborative learning themselves. Teachers spend a great deal of time meeting and planning together. The six teams of teachers meet weekly to plan and discuss curriculum, instruction, individual students or teachers, and other issues. These meeting times are built into their schedules. During the period of our study, Slater's Motion team met formally twice a week for three and a half hours and informally at other times when necessary. They also used the time to conference with students or parents, using a translator (a student or staff member) if needed.

Collaborative Learning

In classrooms at International, the emphasis is on active learning. The entire school employs a student-centered classroom, using small heterogeneous groups. While students work in groups, the teacher takes on the role of facilitator and orchestrator, helping both individuals and groups.

Students aren't grouped according to particular language, age, grade, or achievement levels. This diversity in groups gives novice English language learners many good models to learn from and the opportunity to grow as they work through a unit together.

Speaking one's native tongue is welcomed in groups where novice learners may rely greatly on peers to assist in clarifying language and meaning. Students who share a native language help each other to understand an issue in English. Yet English is the main language at International. It is usually the only common language for students working collaboratively, and it becomes the tool to successfully complete the written and oral requirements for a topic. Students come to see that they need to open English conversations with others in their groups in order to succeed.

Younger students also watch as older students begin preparing their graduation portfolios. Younger students become privy to the college application process and how older students enroll in college classes in the community college that surrounds them. The whole idea of college becomes so ingrained and such a fact of life that once they hit their senior year, the question is not "Will I ever be accepted to college?" but "Which college will I go to?" The school is very successful in numbers of students accepted to college—over 90 percent in 1997–98.

The faculty and staff at International believe they must model the kind of collaborative approach they expect of their students, and they work collaboratively on many levels—within their teams, across teams, and on schoolwide committees. One teacher credits this kind of collaborative working environment with promoting, "first and foremost, a feeling of self-confidence [that] broadens the scope of what [she] can produce." The school is exemplary, too, in that the principal constantly acknowledges and congratulates teachers and students for their successes and extra efforts. He is an exceptional leader and is highly respected.

Mentoring

Mentoring is used to socialize individuals into the International community, to assist them in learning the way the school works as well as in acquiring new ideas. A new student is paired with a student of the same first language so that they can help each other use their native language to continue to do coursework as they also learn English. Teachers mentor students in all their coursework on an ongoing basis; they also mentor students in relation to their portfolios. Newer teachers are mentored by more experienced ones. And all teachers are part of a "peer support team," a small group that includes both newer and more experienced teachers and is designed to give feedback and support to group members. In addition, teams sometimes mentor each other by sharing ideas and providing feedback.

Peer Support and Peer Evaluation Teams

Teachers within each interdisciplinary team interact with each other actively and in a meaningful context. More experienced teachers are able to share their wisdom and experience, while less experienced teachers offer fresh insight. Everyone learns. Within the team, individuals set their own goals and collaborate on team goals.

In addition, all teachers are reviewed by peer evaluation teams (PETs) put together by the Personnel Committee. Nontenured teachers are reviewed annually, and issues of appointment and tenure are discussed. Tenured teachers are reviewed every three years but write a yearly self-evaluation. In the process of review, teachers make a presentation to their peer evaluation team. This is an opportunity for the teachers to discuss their accomplishments and goals for the future. During the year, each teacher keeps a portfolio that includes an administrative evaluation, peer evaluations, self-evaluations, and two class sets of student evaluations for each semester, and this portfolio is reviewed at the PET presentation. (Teachers taught differing numbers of classes, depending on what other jobs they performed for the school. Most teachers, however, taught four.)

The peer evaluation team considers the portfolio, the teacher's presentation of his or her accomplishments and goals for the future, and feedback from the teacher's teaching team. Together, they create a plan for meeting the teacher's goals for the following year. This is a supportive process rather than a judgmental one. (Slater's PET presentation is described later in this chapter.) The entire PET process mirrors to a great extent the presentation that students make at the end of each semester when they present their portfolios, have them reviewed by teachers and peers, and discuss their accomplishments and goals. Eric Nadelstern, principal of International, pointed out that once teachers became comfortable with putting together portfolios and evaluating themselves and peers on the basis of their own public presentations, only then were they ready to offer such a process to their students.

Schoolwide Evaluation

Each year, the school itself conducts an end-of-year evaluation report. In 1996–97, this report reviewed curriculum and instruction, student support services, long- and short-range planning, management of public relations, staff and personnel management, and personal and professional development. It offers evidence that the faculty are involved in thinking about what has worked and what has not; what has been successfully implemented and what needs fine tuning; objectives for the coming year; and a schedule for implementing those objectives.

For example, in the 1996–97 evaluation, one instructional goal was to have 90 percent of candidates for graduation "meet or exceed Regents standards [i.e., standards for the New York State Regents exam] in English, math, science, and social studies as determined by graduation certification panels which will review candidates' portfolios and hear candidates' presentations." It was decided that the school would develop, refine, and pilot rubrics based on those standards in the following year.

Such action clearly shows that the school is constantly striving to improve already commendable graduation rates and is looking at ways to improve the assessment practices already in place. Again, the school as a whole considers goals, past and future, as the road to improvement and development.

Graduation Requirements

Students' progress is constantly monitored, they are given feedback, and they are assisted in preparing performance-based assessment tasks. Once students have successfully completed three years of course work, they each receive a faculty mentor and become a candidate for graduation. To graduate, students must successfully complete a minimum of four years of interdisciplinary study. They must also be certified by a panel including faculty, students, and representatives from the community as part of their petition to graduate. In their fourth year, students are assisted by their mentors in putting together graduation portfolios—which consist of performance-based assessment tasks selected from their coursework plus other pieces of work that show evidence of growth and mastery—and in preparing for their presentations. The graduation certification panels meet during January, June, and August.

Each graduation certification panel meets for about two hours to

- frame questions and discuss the graduation portfolio (without the student present),
- hear the presentation and discuss it with the candidate,
- deliberate and come to consensus on whether the student has met graduation criteria,
- inform the student of the results.

Certification for graduation is based on the consensus of the panel, and the graduation is subject to successful completion of coursework. It is a rigorous undertaking to prepare a graduation portfolio.

Learning a Language

International operates from the belief that literacy learning (reading, writing, speaking, listening, and thinking) occurs in a meaningful context and in a language-rich environment. The classroom focus is on high-quality, in-depth work, rather than on isolated skills. Expectations are high and varied for each student. Novice English language learners are given the same assignments as those who are more experienced. Novices are expected to use the collaborative environment to ask for help from other students and to make use of their native language as an avenue into the collective learning experience. In having to work in a group and to constantly share thoughts and information, students become familiar with the language of sharing and of asking questions, and they begin the journey to becoming skillful communicators in English. As one student, Nikolas, explains:

> When we do an activity, we have to work as a group so somebody definitely understands the question or we cannot solve it. We talk between us and we help each other. . . . It's good to work as a group because you have to talk to them in English, and that's how you learn.

In addition, continued development of their native languages is fundamental to learning. Teachers see themselves as teachers of language as well as content. They have incorporated language development techniques into their teaching, regardless of the subject they teach, and they place high priority on language growth. Teachers work to provide purposeful use of English as well as of the students' native languages. In class, when the teacher is not fluent in the language of the group she or he is assisting, she or he discusses the material in English. Students may return to their native languages when the teacher leaves. If they need more assistance, the teacher helps students locate the resources they need. The focus on native language development at International has also fostered the development of relationships between the school and the students' ethnolinguistic communities. International supports its students with a variety of native-language materials, an effort supported in part by an Improved School Services grant from the state.

Evidence of Success at International High School

The school strives to lessen the existing gap of achievement between immigrant students and native speakers of English. It has won many national and state awards and compares more than favorably with similar inner-city schools in terms of student achievement. For example:

- In 1995–96, 65.4 percent of students in New York City achieved mandated gains in English-language proficiency. At International, 70.5 percent of students achieved mandated gains in English language proficiency.

- In 1996–97, 93 percent of all International students passed all classes. In New York City, two-thirds of students fail one of their classes, and almost half fail more than one of their classes.

- In New York City, 48.45 percent of the class of 1997 graduated after just four years of high school, with 35.7 percent still enrolled; 15.9 percent had dropped out. International High School, on the other hand, saw 66.7 percent of students graduate after four years of high school, while 33.3 percent were still enrolled, and 0 percent had dropped out.

- International has a very low dropout rate—1.7 percent of those who entered ninth grade in 1992 and tenth grade in 1993 dropped out. In New York City overall, the dropout rate for similar students was 16.4 percent.

- In 1997, the attendance rate was 95.1 percent at International, while in similar New York schools overall it was 85.7 percent.

- In 1996–97, 91.8 percent of International students were accepted to a two- or four-year college. This compares with 85.6 percent of students going on to some form of postsecondary education (kind not specified) from across the whole of New York City.

International High School has been on the cutting edge of reform and innovation since its inception in 1985. Its personnel procedures, peer evaluation, peer hiring, and peer support strategies have been adopted in the Board's contract with the United Federation of Teachers as a school-based option for all public schools in New York City. The United States Department of Education has awarded International an Academic Excellence Dissemination grant for two three-year periods, from 1992–95 and 1996–99. In 1998, International received the National Award for Model Professional Development from the U.S. Department of Education. In 1992, Marsha Slater received the New York State English Council Teacher of Excellence Award. In 1989, principal Eric Nadelstern received the Distinguished Service Award from the state chapter of TESOL (Teachers of English to Speakers of Other Languages). The school hosts over a thousand visitors a year, and news articles about the school have appeared in many publications, including the *New York Times*, *New York Newsday*, the *Daily News*, and *Harvard Educational Review*.

Special Programs

Because newly arrived immigrants can be overwhelmed by personal, economic, and adjustment issues, International provides a strong support system to students and their parents. The school maintains links with its community by offering, for example, ESL classes to parents. It also gives information on college enrollment, financial aid, and health insurance. Parents come to see the caring nature of the school and the warm embrace it offers their children.

In 1997–98, the school changed its approach to guidance. Previously, Personnel Services (Guidance) worked out of centralized offices behind closed doors; counselors would be consulted by school faculty when necessary. Now, however, each team includes a guidance counselor, who teaches one class four days a week and devotes the remaining time to providing support for students and parents, including helping with college applications. Now that guidance counselors are on every team, students feel more connected in ways that eliminate anonymity. Principal Nadelstern applauded the change as enormously beneficial, and said that by the end of March 1998 there had not been a single suspension all year, whereas "three years ago we had thirty, two years ago we had fifteen, last year we had ten." Slater has become the guidance counselor for her team.

When a student is having problems in class, another student may be hired to help tutor the student. Money is set aside in each team's budget for this purpose, and it is entirely a team issue to decide which student needs the support. Often a student who speaks the same native language will work with the struggling student.

Wednesday afternoons are set aside for student clubs—including the International Club, Live Music Club, Latino Club, Chinese Club, and Sports Club—as well as seminars on the PSAT/SAT. The clubs give students the opportunity to make new friends, enjoy old ones, and share culture and language. Clubs organize films, lunches, dances, concerts, trips, and presentations.

International students have full access to LaGuardia Community College's facilities, including the library, computer rooms, gymnasium, pool, and cafeterias. Usually by their junior year students can opt to take college classes, and International faculty assist students with enrollment. International faculty also meet with LaGuardia faculty to discuss writing, expectations, and problems in college courses. College faculty are sometimes invited to help in teaching part of a course at International, and some International teachers also teach at the college.

International is linked with two other high schools (all associated with LaGuardia Community College) in a career education program that combines a rigorous curriculum with internships that place students in government agencies, businesses, schools, hospitals, and nonprofit institutions around the city. An internship experience is part of International's graduation requirements. The interns work, usually without pay, for academic credit and work experience. In 1996–97, students worked thirteen weeks, four hours a day, four days a week. The schools have published a comprehensive index of organizations willing to take interns, specifying the position available, travel directions, a brief description of the organization, qualifications needed, and responsibilities of the position. At the conclusion of the internship, students develop an internship album.

Wide Professional Networks

International has a number of important links with other high schools that are located in the area and/or that adopt similar philosophies (e.g., Manhattan, Queens, and Brooklyn International High Schools and Middle College High School). For example, it is a member of the Coalition of Essential Schools.

It is also part of the Alternative High Superintendency of New York City. This group of smaller high schools tends to target particular student populations and have specific foci. These schools are often granted waivers from city and state requirements. For example,

International has a waiver allowing the school to hire teachers outside the United Federation of Teachers (UFT) rules and regulations as well as (at the time of our study) a waiver from requiring students to take New York State's Regents exams.

Within the framework of the Alternative High Schools, there is a partnership between three schools: International High School and two others established in 1993 and 1994. All three provide a multicultural, alternative educational environment, and all serve limited-English-proficiency student populations. The two newer schools are modeled after International.

Regular contact among faculty at the three partnership schools encourages professional growth in mutually supportive ways. Teachers share ideas and target energies toward specific reform. For example, the Partnership schools have met frequently to discuss the new state standards. Faculty and administrators from the three schools participated in a three-day retreat in March 1997 to create viable performance-based assessments, because it's "the best chance for LEP kids to have a world-class education," says Nadelstern. Each school brought a list of performance-based assessment tasks that met or exceeded state and national standards. At the retreat, they created a master list and then broke into heterogeneous groups composed of faculty and administrators from each school to tackle the following tasks: (1) compile performance-based assessment tasks for the matrix; (2) determine how and when to assess student work; and (3) decide "how good is good enough," i.e., develop rubrics.

The Teacher

Marsha Slater is one of the founding teachers at International High School. When asked for a metaphor of herself as a teacher, she offers this: "being an adult but seeing the world through the eyes of a child, like E. E. Cummings." She holds master's degrees in anthropology and in education administration and supervision and completed her Ph.D. in English education in 1994. She has been teaching for twenty-nine years, mostly English, and has served as an associate professor at New York University. She has tremendous professional experience as a workshop leader, teacher trainer, and New York City Writing Project course coordinator. She has presented at numerous conferences locally and out of state—for example, she has made presentations at five national conferences of the National Council of Teachers of English (NCTE). She has also made presentations at local universities and colleges. In 1992 she won the New York State English Council's "Teacher of Excellence" award, and she has also won fellowships and grants such as an NCTE research grant and an NEH fellowship at Dartmouth. In addition, Slater has published widely. Clearly her professional career is marked by excellence and extraordinary achievements. But Slater does not sit on her laurels; she continues in a lifelong learning mode.

Slater acknowledges that she experienced a pivotal change in her teaching while she was involved in the New York City Writing Project more than halfway through her career. Before doing this project, she had believed that the teacher's role is to transmit knowledge to students. She saw herself as a good teacher, was mentoring others constantly, and was winning awards for her teaching. She says that "all I had ever experienced or been told or known, was transmission teaching":

> [I] thought that I was doing the students good when I sat with my feet up and a red pen in my hand for seventeen years in a row marking book reports or essays, weekend after weekend after weekend. . . . After years and years and years and years of doing that and seeing almost no carryover between the red pen marks on the paper and the way they wrote their next composition . . . for me the real eye-opener was the New York City Writing Project. . . . I was totally transformed from being burned out and wanting to leave.

She also took a couple of Writing Project residential courses in London and Oxford with Nancy Martin, James Britton, and Pat Barrett. Her intense interest in theory and learning encouraged her to begin a Ph.D., for which her research focused on a mathematics teacher's explorations of writing-to-learn with limited-English-proficiency students. She considers reflective thinking and practice as well as theory to be the biggest influences on her professional life:

> When I was in the [New York City] Writing Project, we read theory and practiced theory. We experienced theory. I saw the connection, and then I was hungry for more theory to change my practice because I was dissatisfied with my practice.

Slater is a member of professional organizations such as NCTE and subscribes to several professional journals. She has done the circuit of conferences, both as presenter and as listener, and has come to believe that her own knowledge and experience hold validity and richness. She constantly reflects on her practice. She has been instrumental in introducing the writing-to-learn approach in the school, and peers respect and seek out her experience and knowledge. She has chaired the Curriculum Committee at International for a number of years.

Reflection and Evaluation in Slater's Professional Experience

As discussed above, teachers at International keep portfolios and are reviewed by peer evaluation teams (PETs) composed of teachers from throughout the school. In 1997, Slater, a tenured teacher, presented her portfolio to her PET. The portfolio revealed the importance of reflection in Slater's professional growth and showed the extent to which she reflects on how things play out in the classroom as well as looks forward and sets goals. Here are some statements from her self-evaluation:

> This year I have consciously made major changes in my professional life. . . . Last year I taught ninety preservice teachers four hours a week over the course of the year at NYU. . . . I decided for my sanity and health not to repeat it this year. . . . While in the throes of that decision, I was given two alternatives: (1) I was approached by R. T. to work with a team of two . . . student teachers for the year, and (2) Judith Langer at SUNY Albany asked me to participate in a two-year observational/interview study in English/language arts learning and the professional growth of English teachers. I chose to do both. . . . Both experiences have made me examine my daily practice, my theory in action, my beliefs and reflective routines.

> . . . [I]t is invaluable to be able to reflect on practice with [the SUNY research assistant] in-depth, as I did at the Partnership retreat in March. . . . By trying to construct a coherent picture for her of the influences on my practice, my theoretical underpinnings, the reasoning behind my pedagogical decisions, I got to deconstruct and reconstruct some of my own understandings of my professional life.

> . . . [B]ecause I was required to put formal student evaluations in my portfolio, I had the opportunity to ask our students to give me written feedback. . . .

> . . . I have folded [my two student teachers] into the evaluation process. Since they have been with me on a steady basis since October, who better to write my peer evaluation?

> . . . I have learned to welcome support and have come to rely on feedback and considerable team work.

> . . . For me, teaching isn't about getting information into someone else's head. It's about watching someone learn to take responsibility for himself and others. It's about enabling and cajoling others to discover and follow their bliss. It's about that '80s word—empowerment.

And on her team:

> . . . If we continue to get activity essays and final topic essays which make trivial connections and show superficial under-

standing of the topic and the themes of the course, then we must rethink how we teach. We may need to rewrite activity guides to include questions specifically designed to create a scaffolded dialogue within the group and again during the mastery question debriefing specifically on the subtopic concept.

Slater's two student teachers included the following statements:

> To work with Marsha is to get inside her mind, to expose yourself to real issues, to take a walk along the same shore with a peer thick in the theory and practice of teaching, sharing, everything. . . .

> . . . [M]ost of her comments to and conversations with the students [about assessment] are used to focus students on their thinking processes, to guide them to make connections between the activities, the subtopics and topics of the semester, and their lives. This way of assessing is very beneficial to the students because it gives them a sense of where they are in the learning process.

> . . . Marsha is a reflective person—it certainly shows in her practice—and she was gracious enough to reflect aloud, which was probably the best way for me to be introduced to teaching and learning.

Slater's portfolio not only gave her the opportunity to reflect on herself as a teacher, peer, and team member; it also highlights the networked sharing that is encouraged by such a process. As a teacher, Slater is linked to a wider community of students, student teachers, team teachers, and teachers from other teams. She is invited by the wider community to share her strengths, as well as her perceptions of areas for growth or concern.

The protocol for the peer evaluation team at International is for the panel members and visitors to read the teacher's portfolio and agree upon questions to ask. The teacher is then invited to give a short presentation. During Slater's presentation, one of the peer evaluators was intrigued with her discussion of metacognitive journals. He asked for and received a thorough explanation of how she used them with her students, and she gave him guidelines she had written for students. He said he was now going to restructure the way he used journals in his classroom to reflect Slater's model, as well as share these ideas with his interdisciplinary team. Later, another peer evaluator said that Slater's comments about working as a team validated her own thoughts and experiences. All of the teachers involved in Slater's peer review—Slater and the peer evaluators—felt professionally nourished by the experience.

Slater's peer evaluation took place within the context of a school whose personnel procedures state:

> If we view ourselves as effective educators, we must also view ourselves as learners. We are role models for our students. If we model authority, our students will learn to be authoritarian. If we model self-improvement in an atmosphere of sharing, that is what our students will learn.

Slater's Work on Her Team

Each of International's six teams of teachers meets regularly to work on issues of curriculum, instruction, concern about individual students or teachers, and other crucial issues. Slater is part of the Motion team. The team's interdisciplinary themes for the two semesters are "Motion" and "Visibility/Invisibility." According to Slater, "The way my team works is professional development!" Despite the team's formal schedule of meeting twice weekly for three and a half hours, supplemented by informal meetings when necessary, a common complaint is that there is never enough time to sit and plan.

The Motion team made some curricular changes for the fall 1997 semester based on their reflections on the previous year's classes, such as deciding to increase the emphasis on research papers. During the previous semester, the team had made extensive curricular changes based on their evaluations of students' portfolios, mastery statements, and comments. Among these changes, several writing activities were added—for example, science logs, daily metacognitive journals, additional essays, literature letters, and portfolio reviews conducted twice a semester in small peer groups with at least two teachers present.

When necessary, the teachers meet with students to discuss issues of concern regarding their work. The whole team sits with the student at issue, being supportive on the one hand, yet collectively finding ways to resolve or minimize the problem at hand, be it tardiness or not completing work.

At one particular meeting, a father was invited in as the team was concerned about his son's lack of work, despite repeated conversations with the student. The meeting was wholly supportive, and the parent, with limited English, spoke through a translator, a family worker from the front office. This lengthy conversation with the parent resulted in a marked improvement in the work ethic of the student, which he and others commented on in his conference at the end of the year. The team genuinely cares about students, and, even more important, it acts when necessary.

Team meetings are a time when the teachers share ideas, bring in materials they think may be useful to others, or simply ask for input on particular issues. Teachers also use team time to reflect on goals and accomplishments and to strive for improvement. The team always meets in Slater's room, which has a computer, so they can write up the new portfolio cover sheets for students or list team goals. Slater sits at the helm and types while the team offers input. There is no leader or head of department; everyone contributes substantively and equally. Yet clearly Slater is revered as the most experienced member and the one who has been mentoring two of the newer team members. The team supports and nurtures its teachers and helps if problems arise. The team also supports several student teachers and looks forward to their help and input in the classroom. In 1997 the team had five student teachers.

The Motion team has undergone significant change in the last few years. Tony Brachman, who originally developed the "Motion" curriculum, had been a charismatic member of the team until 1996, when he retired. His absence caused a vacuum at first but eventually resulted in some progressive changes for the team. For example, the curricular changes mentioned above have strengthened the program significantly. Most of these changes stem from Slater, who had been reluctant to suggest substantive curricular changes when Tony was a member of the team, since they were such good friends. In a peer evaluation written for her portfolio, one of Slater's student teachers describes how Slater became more of a leader on the team:

> Marsha has taken a leadership role in the team this year, working closely with her fellow team members. The team as a whole has taken the initiative to examine how they can better help the students toward deeper, more meaningful understanding of the subject matter. Marsha provided many of the ideas the team discussed and eventually implemented, and helped the team to examine the feasibility of all suggestions by drawing from her experiences and the conclusions they have led her to. This was especially so when the conversations turned to using writing more effectively throughout the curriculum. (Charles 5/22/97)

The Classroom: How Students Experience English

Slater's classroom is a relaxed yet busy place. The small windowless room is crammed with cupboards, tables and chairs in permanent groups, and students. Slater refers to the room as a "human sandwich." Students are usually working in groups on activity guides while Slater keeps a low profile, moving from group to group. It all appears to work effortlessly, yet Slater's every move seems to have a purpose.

During one classroom observation, students were working in their groups on the activity guide for the poem "Southbound on the Freeway." Everything in this lesson seemed to be moving by itself, students were on task, and lots and lots of talk was going on. What might have looked like a lack of teacher control was, in fact, student activity framed by explicit expectations on the part of the teacher—all were to use their groups to move their understandings forward, the activity guide had to be finished, and if groups were ready to debrief they had to indicate this to Slater. Students were asking questions and going back to the poem.

Slater began by sitting with one group, explaining how language is learned: that just as students do experiments in science, so language learning means making mistakes. She quietly talked with another student, Anna, regarding the literature letter she had written to her partner. Anna had written a summary instead of responding to the book and giving her opinion. Slater was upping the ante and telling Anna about what more needed to go in the letter. Meanwhile, in another group, Cheng, a complete beginner in English, used an electronic dictionary to plod through translating the poem word for word, conversing in Chinese with Wei, a sophomore. Manuel suddenly invited Wei into the group conversation: "How is poetry different to stories and newspapers?" Wei replied quietly: "This has rhythm." In yet another group, Maria was explaining how a news article is written differently, and at one point turned to a specific group member and asked in Spanish how to say "rima" ("rhyme") in English.

On the top of the front wall of Slater's room hangs a slogan printed by a previous student: "Give a man a fish and you feed him for a day; teach him how to fish and you feed him for a lifetime." Slater spent time quietly relating the slogan to a student who wanted to know how to spell a word. She told him that if he learned how to strategize spelling, to look for patterns over time, he would learn to spell the word and teach it to himself. But if she just told him how to spell the word, it would be like giving him a fish.

Slater is guided by patience. When students clearly don't understand and their group can't help them, she talks one-on-one with them and gives them time to sift through things. The process of acculturation takes time—it can take time to get used to the other students and to the patterns and rhythms of this classroom.

Slater feels that in order for students to learn language, they "need to swim in it." In her classroom, students are truly immersed in talk, literature, reading, writing, and thinking, which together form a rich language environment. Anyone familiar with the typical scenario of an ESL classroom—students silently working through a worksheet, vocabulary words first, then low-level comprehension questions to test their understanding or lack thereof—would be amazed at the way in which these ESL students were talking purposefully and seriously about this poem, trying to tease it apart.

In order to give a full sense of how English is experienced in Slater's class, the important components of this classroom's English instruction are discussed below: student groups, student talk, writing, reading, thinking, and assessment.

Student Groups

Slater strongly believes that group work serves as the basis of learning. Students need language to manage and organize their groups and also to develop understandings and interpretations of what they read. They can choose to use their native language, if there are other speakers in the group, but clearly English is the language of choice, if one is to succeed as part of the group.

Slater has a deep-down trust in her students' ability to figure things out for themselves, whether it be spelling patterns, genre issues, comprehension, or vocabulary. She insists that students think about their questions first on their own and with their group. If students come to her with a question, she asks, "Have you asked your group?" Slater know she is not the only holder of knowledge, and she encourages students to find the language to ask questions of the group, and then to construct their answers.

Composition of Groups

Throughout the school, small heterogeneous groups of students of all grades (9–12) engage in projects for which they construct knowledge with careful coaching by the teacher. At the beginning of each new topic, Slater sets time aside for regrouping, when students choose new groups. Importance is attached to the selection process, as students come to realize that their work will be affected by all students cooperating and working effectively together. Slater's rules for forming groups are: (1) no more than two speakers of the same language, and (2) a balance of gender, language experience, and age.

The heterogeneity of groups sees older and younger students working together, learning from each other. The older students serve as models, as what Vygotsky (1978) called "the more knowledgeable other." Students with greater language proficiency provide leadership within the group, modeling ways to participate, ways to discuss, and ways to think. Slater applauds heterogeneity:

> I just keep my ears open to how they're doing in their groups. I mean that's one of the great things about having older students, because they do take the new ones under their wing and show them the ropes, and every kid has figured out how to work in a group, where to go for help. We watch from a safe distance to let them figure it out and gain the confidence themselves, and do as little spoon-feeding as possible.

Learning to Participate in a Group

Students come to International bringing their school experiences from their native countries, as well as some experience from attending American schools. Most seem not to have experienced a school where group work forms the basis of learning. This is a big adjustment. Slater is aware of the extra scaffolding needed at the beginning of the year to help "students [who are] feeling their way through things." This is the time when they ask a lot of logistical questions. Slater, however, trusts her notions of learning, and, even more, she trusts her students: "The whole structure has to sink in for them first."

Students are given tremendous freedom, which comes with learning to be responsible for their learning, and clearly it takes time for new students to adjust. Thomas, a first-year student, took a long while to settle into purposeful group work, preferring instead to play and joke around. While he had no other speaker of his native languages (French and Lingala), he was also inexperienced in speaking English. Rosa, the natural leader in the group, often tried to bring order, and she later commented:

> I am like the babysitter of Thomas. Now I don't care to do that, you know, because I want the best for him, you know, and not just for him, for my own group, because my grades depend on all the people who are in my group. . . . He's changed a lot. He's very quiet now. Now he's more interested in his work and I feel so proud of him.

Another student suddenly blossomed in the late winter after students didn't want to include her in their group on regrouping day. Slater spoke to her privately about the "subtext" of that painful ostracism. She realized that her lack of effort and laziness stood in her way, and in the next topic she thrust herself headlong into focused group work. She emerged as a leader, and shone when she took a novice student under her own wing.

Given the heterogeneous nature of the groups, novice students have ample opportunity to learn group dynamics simply by looking to older or more experienced students. Slater admits that the older students are good models because "they've figured out their priorities and they tell the other kids to stop fooling around and to get to work."

Students learn to juggle the tensions and balances within the group with regard to personal identity, group connectedness, and the balance of individuality and connectedness (Langer, 1995). Tension in a group needs to be not only recognized but also articulated by group members. Many times during the year, individuals expressed frustration and exasperation with group members who hadn't completed their work by the deadline the group had set. For example, in December, one group was ready to debrief, and found that Ju-Xing was still not finished, even though they had already given him a two-day extension:

Manuel:	Ju-Xing, you finished?
Ju-Xing:	[Shakes his head and looks down.]
Manuel:	[To the others:] He didn't finish the activity. We all did it and he's the only one who haven't finished it.
Maria:	[To Ju-Xing:] Have you finished this?
Ju-Xing:	[Shakes head and looks down.]
Maria:	[To the others:] He told me he was going to finish it for today. She's not gonna debrief us if you're not finished. Jesus Christ, come on Ju-Xing. Come on, we're depending on you. [Maria continues to express frustration in English, then vent in Spanish with Manuel.] You haven't finished?
Payal:	We are going to start doing the learning log?
Maria:	I'm going to start because we cannot do Motion. He haven't finished.
Payal:	We can if we like help him finish the activity.
Maria:	I have helped him. I have told him.
Manuel:	[To Ju-Xing:] I have given you my activity.
Payal:	What if he don't finish it tomorrow either?
Manuel:	We could just start another activity. We could just start it.

Maria:	We talk with Marsha and tell her . . . we cannot do anything here because of this. Why don't we talk with Marsha and tell her to debrief us and then she could debrief us because we're really losing time. OK you gonna be the one who's gonna call her?
Manuel:	Me?
Payal:	Okay I'll call her, and you explain like what you want to do.
Manuel:	Okay, okay. I call her, you whisper.
Maria:	[Vents in Spanish with Manuel.] He's gotta accept what's going on you know. We're gonna be stuck in this. Miss [to Slater] we want to debrief! He's not finished. We have told him two days, but we are here, we are ready to debrief, and he's not finished so we want you to debrief us.

Several things are interesting about the conversation above. We can see students adopting and negotiating various roles—who will call the teacher? Students openly express their frustration at Ju-Xing. Some float ideas about what to do—start new work or debrief now. It is clear that these students have learned to function as a group. All members of the group must finish work by the date they determine together, and, if things go astray, it is the group's task to try resolving the problem. They have learned how to discuss issues that are important to them. We get a clear sense of community—the group chastises Ju-Xing for not fulfilling the role expected of him. The conversation also points to something remarkable: while traditional ESL classes spend a great deal of time drilling verb tenses, here, students purposefully use a whole host of verb tenses, in context.

The Students as Teachers

Slater believes that "if there are twenty-four students in the class, then there are twenty-five teachers." More experienced language users take on the role of teachers for the less experienced, who, over time, become teachers themselves. Within the intimate group setting, students feel comfortable asking questions and helping each other. It is less threatening and involves less risk taking than does speaking out in a larger group.

Developing a Community

Over time, the group, and then the whole class, grow to be safe environments where the novice student sees there are others struggling for words or confounded by a piece of literature. As trust and relationships develop, a community evolves. Students come to see how this community benefits them. As shown above, students transform through participation in activities of their group, and activities of their community (Rogoff, 1994). They have learned ways to behave, to participate in a group, and to use the knowledge gained to move themselves forward into different roles. Both Thomas and Erica stopped playing around and focused on their work, and the group that was annoyed at Ju-Xing for not finishing his work felt empowered when they successfully convinced Slater that she should debrief them without Ju-Xing, who had not done his part despite their helping him and giving him more time. For his part, Ju-Xing learned firsthand the consequences of not fulfilling his role in the group.

Student Talk

It is easy for an observer to take the group talk in Slater's classroom for granted. Student talk is an inherent and natural part of learning—the glue that holds everything else together (reading, writing, and thinking). That is certainly not the case in many other high school classrooms, where even students in mainstream classrooms get to talk very little (Nystrand, Gamoran, & Carbonaro, 1998). Speakers of languages other than English actually get *even less* opportunity to talk in class (Arreaga-Mayer & Perdomo-Rivera, 1996). Very little authentic talk occurs in the run-of-the-mill ESL class, at any level. In looking for clues as to why Slater's is an exemplary classroom, one factor stands out: classroom discourse is valued and used as a tool.

Learning How to Participate in Discussions

As shown above, students quickly learn social rules and appropriate language for discussion—how to enter a discussion, question, respond, challenge, and disagree. They also learn ways to discuss literature. Because Slater's class works in groups, each group finds its own way of working through a piece of literature, but all are scaffolded by teacher-prepared activity guides, which offer questions to be considered. The activity guide leads the group through central issues related to the literature and therefore guides, in a macro way, their group discussion. Before reading the short story "To Build a Fire," for example, students had a prereading question to answer:

> "The more you move the longer you live." Discuss with your group and decide what you think this sentence means about people physically and mentally. Each person should write the answers in his or her own words.

This question focused the group on trying to understand the saying. Later, once they had read the story, the group members were directed to write down any questions they had and discuss them with the group. Another series of questions focused on a plot summary, the ending, the conflict, and the theme, leading students to consider and understand the genre. The activity guide also asks four "mastery questions" that get to the philosophical and conceptual ideas of the story, and students must answer these for debriefing. (See Appendix D for a sample activity guide.)

While the activity guide might sound restrictive and teacher-dominated to some, the thrust of group discussion centers on students' own questions, in relation to the bigger teacher-chosen questions. Most students were confused about exactly what happened in certain parts of "To Build a Fire."

For example, in one group, Esperanza said, "I don't get this here. The man wants to go to the gold mine there. I don't get it. I don't know why he say that." Payal and Manuel immediately hopped in to help her. Payal pointed Esperanza to the exact part of the text that helped her, and then she consulted with Manuel in Spanish to see if "mine" is "la mina." The conversation faded, but then Manuel piped up: "Who's Jack London?" Later, Maria asked, "How you feel about the end?" This conversation was typical of the way students had their own agendas as they worked through the activity guide. They were guided by it, but they also jumped to the aid of other students who needed help. Effective investigation depended on effective use of discourse: where the question had to be formed, confidence had to be mustered to ask it, and then a break in the conversation had to be recognized to finally state the question.

This conversation is interesting, too, because it shows how students weave in and out of different orientations toward understanding the story (Langer, 1992). All the time, the ESL student seems alert to gaining specific information: What does this word mean? What is this word in English/Spanish? What does this idiom mean? How is this word spelled? Langer calls this seeking of information "a point of reference orientation."

When readers engage in a literary experience, their orientation can be called reaching toward a "horizon of possibilities" (Langer, 1995). In such an orientation, the reader explores the possibilities of the text as it is read, and understandings may change as the story unfolds. The focus is on developing a personal interpretation. This orientation does not occur all the time in Slater's class, because much of the group talk centers on a point-of-reference orientation, where students are figuring out the basic meanings of what they read.

Slater pushes them, however, to engage further in a literary experience through the mastery questions in the activity guide. These mastery questions are discussed orally in the debriefing, in writing in the essays that connect ideas across interdisciplinary lines, and in individual conversations that students have with Slater. The conventional recitation structure for classroom participation, where only the teacher has power to ask questions and the student has an obligation to answer them correctly, has no place here.

The talk that Slater uses in class is in itself real (that is, authentic, in that it deals with issues the students raise about their understandings of the text) and articulate. Many people, teachers included, feel they need to speak slowly and simplify their language when talking with students who speak a language other then English (and often that means talking loudly, too). Yet as Slater debriefs a group on their reading and discussion of "To Build a Fire," she doesn't simplify her language as she recounts what students have said so far. Instead, she encourages them to think more deeply: "You're using the text to help you understand, exactly. So (he) ignores the journey partially because he has no imagination, partially because he's incredibly stubborn, all right. He wants to do what he wants to do. What do you think his going on the journey anyway says about human beings?" The language she uses could easily be part of an exemplary mainstream classroom group discussion. She does not water it down. Her assumption is that students understand, and if they don't, they'll ask or figure it out.

Learning to discuss within the group prepares one for the debriefing experience in which she wants students to talk about their understandings of the literature. The debriefing discussion prepares students for their participation in the more public grade conference twice a semester. In their grade conferences, each student talks about his or her learning to date, and about what he or she is proud of. Teachers and peers give their reflections and assessments of the student's learning, and the student learns to defend and perhaps challenge a grade or comment given. This all leads to the final graduation portfolio meeting in the senior year, where, as described above, the student gives a presentation and answers questions from a committee.

One of the crucial gains of centering learning on community is the gradual development of voice in the student, an academic voice that is specific to situations such as debriefing, grade conferences, and the graduation conference. It is as though the student earns his or her *academic clothing* in this rite of passage from the small beginnings in the group to a powerful presentation for graduation. Academic language is made explicit. Students learn the importance of academic clothing: look confident, look your audience in the eye, speak assertively, speak clearly, speak intelligently, think critically. An example of a student who gained this academic clothing is Nina, a Spanish-speaking beginner, who sat timidly and quietly at first, eyes glued to the text. For over a semester, other Spanish speakers sat and translated with her. Gradually, she started to ask quiet vocabulary questions, her writing increased in bulk, and she began to make eye contact, and then Erica befriended her. From there on, Nina blossomed, and Slater proudly announced at the end of the spring semester, "You know that Nina went and challenged Jackie (a humanities teacher), about her essay grade!" Nina realized the power of voice, of speaking up; she had listened and watched all those months, and she seized the opportunity to speak up when she felt insulted by a low grade for a project she had worked so hard on. Nina and others take this ability to develop a voice with them to college and the outside world, where they have to use English in order to do things such as seek help, find a job, advocate for self or family, negotiate grades, challenge decisions, and articulate confidently. Students at International learn how to be successful and how to present a public self. Day in, day out, Slater's classroom provides a rich language environment where students are expected to be actively involved in the curriculum, using either English or their native language. Nina spent much time in figuring out how the classroom worked (what was expected, how to complete activity guides and portfolios, how a group works, how to ask for help). Slater gave her time to "figure it out."

Personal Talk

Social studies and science often float naturally in and out of conversations in Slater's class, as students make connections with the interdisciplinary approach. Another genre of talk that finds its way into Slater's class is of a personal and social nature. This is the "coffee talk," in which students talk about personal information, all apparently "off task." Yolanda talks about her boyfriend/mother problem, Anna tells how her employer rounds off to the nearest dollar and omits twenty-four cents of her pay each week, and Alejandro talks about the violent acts and images he finds in the music he likes.

All this "chitchat" is an important part of friendship and community building and draws the most unlikely students together. Slater, too, bonds with her students by joining in conversations, telling of the boyfriend who never bought flowers, and how she wears socks in bed in the winter. Slater explicitly shows that personal sharing of information has its place here. This is the stuff that builds the fires of friendship and creates a sense of community. Students from different language backgrounds use English as the common language to build friendships. Language is used and learned through this personal talk, which invites people into the conversation.

Native Language

Students' native languages have a legitimate place in Slater's classroom. Books in various languages cram her cupboards, as do dictionaries. These books make a student's native language visible, thus raising its status and giving it validity. Students may choose books in their native language for their literature letters, and complete beginners can write their responses to the activity guide in their native language as long as they then translate what they have written. In contrast, most ESL classrooms check the native languages at the door with the coats.

Thus a student's native language is legitimized as an appropriate resource for learning in this exemplary class (Bakhtin, 1981). Many students, beginners and veterans alike, flash back and forth between their native language and English. It is a quick way of confirming the meaning or spelling of a word. Rosa says: "You know it's good to ask in Spanish, so that I can understand better." Native language is used to develop meaning and comprehension and to confirm understandings. For example, in discussing "To Build a Fire," Manuel suddenly quips in Spanish that the man did not die. He then converses simultaneously with Payal in English and Maria in Spanish, asking for evidence of death. He's finally convinced but not until he finds the exact moment of death, when the students do a close word-for-word reading of the text. Manuel uses Spanish both to get to the core of his question and to work out the details. Other languages are commonly used in this class to work out understandings. Students also use their native languages to form friendships and talk about personal and everyday issues.

In their portfolios, students must write letters to their parents in their native languages and also translate into English the replies from their parents. Using one's native language does not impede the learning of English; rather, it supports it. Novice English language learners, in particular, rely on talking in their native language as "a way in" both to the group conversation and to learning English. They themselves determine their transitioning to English. While Slater can encourage from the sidelines, and group members may nudge, too, ultimately it's up to them to make the moves. From feeling awkward, isolated, and afraid to talk, these students are given the time and space to develop their voices.

In this exemplary class, talk has a central role in learning language and in learning content. It is the tool for getting ahead and for success. Students learn ways to discuss and to enter conversations, and they learn that they must talk in order for their questions and concerns to be addressed. They learn to dance between their native languages and English, using one to support the other.

In nurturing the classroom community, Slater creates boundless opportunities for talk. She offers engaging and often provocative literature for students to read, and she insists that students develop understandings for themselves. It is this search for meaning that gives students much reason to talk.

Writing

Students swim in a rich language environment here, where many good writing models and writing prompts are provided. Although students in typical U.S. schools don't do much extended writing (Nystrand, Gamoran & Carbonaro, 1998), International High School students do extended writing constantly.

As mentioned earlier, Slater has been part of the New York City Writing Project since 1985, and she credits this association for her adoption of group work and of a writing-process approach in her classroom. She does not deal with writing as an isolated activity; rather it is part of the deliberate multilayering of genres, of metacognitive thinking, and of reading, talking, and listening. Students write activity guides, journals, research papers, literature letters, essays, portfolio responses, and other creative pieces. They use writing in a number of ways: for information and understanding; for literary response and expression; for critical analysis and evaluation; and for social interaction.

By writing answers to activity guide questions, students learn to use writing to make their initial thinking and understandings visible. After students have orally debriefed with Slater and discussed the mastery questions from the activity guide, they hand in their activity guides to be marked. She responds in writing and hands them back, usually to be "redone" and resubmitted for credit. Her purpose is to get students to think more deeply about what they have read. Her notes frequently ask students to explain their answers further. Slater also asks students to create their own activity guides that could be used by other students in later years. Students must also write various types of essays that link what they are learning across the disciplines or that integrate what they have learned from their journal writing, research, and reading. Essays need to be turned in on computer disks; it is the students' responsibility to find the college computer rooms and ask for help to learn how to use them.

Students also keep metacognitive journals for writing about what they are learning. Slater was instrumental in introducing metacognitive journals to her team, based on her tremendous belief in the power of writing. She created "The Metacognitive Journal: A Place to Reflect" for students to use as a springboard for their journal writing. She begins this guide with a brief paragraph about why writing is a powerful way of thinking.

The metacognitive journals are written by each student at the end of the school day, no matter which teacher is teaching at that time. That teacher consistently collects, reads, and responds to the journal. When Maria wrote, "I'm not feeling good in my group. . . . [W]e are not working the way I expected, it's just that we all write for our selfs and sometimes we don't even share ideas," she opened an opportunity for discussion that could nudge the group along. The teacher responded, "Esperanza said the same thing in her diary about the group not working enough together—maybe you should bring it up." This example is typical of how the students are truly made to be responsible for their learning. If they have a problem, they need to find the words and the right moment to deal with it themselves.

The following are samples of student comments about their daily journal writing. Kristen, who has demonstrated a great deal of language growth in a short span of time, talked about journal writing in an interview:

> I think that the daily journal helped me a lot, because I was writing about what I did every day. So I could learn new vocabulary, because I could look in the dictionary for new words that I didn't know before. So I think that helped me the most.

Salim is from Syria, where he learned English. He has been in the United States about ten months, and his English is nearly fluent. He said that of all the English activities, he found the daily journals to be the most helpful and also the most difficult.

Milan is from Bosnia and discussed what had helped him learn English. He compared how he learns when he writes freely to how he learns when he completes activity guide questions:

> Maybe it's writing because when you are writing a short story, you are building sentences on your own and you don't have any questions to answer. You have to choose the way to do it by yourself.

In addition, students write "literature letters" each week. They read a chapter of a novel or a short story of their choice and write about what they've read to a chosen partner. The letter is supposed to discuss relationships between the story and the conceptual theme of the course, as well as connections to their own lives and the world around them. In addition, they write responses to their partners' weekly letters. Partners pick the same story so that students gain a visceral sense of the fact that there are multiple possible interpretations of a given text. Students need to work out the perfunctory aspects of the literature letters themselves, such as whom to pick as a partner and on which day to exchange letters.

Mechanics and Grammar

Mechanics and grammar are attended to in context, when a problem arises. Students in this class do not work through worksheets. Traditional notions of "functional literacy" placed heavy emphasis on command of grammar and conventions in ESL and remedial classes. International, however, provides a rich language environment in which students are expected to do extended writing and to focus on developing ideas and meanings. Students hear and use the correct grammar and conventions of English daily. Slater attends to individual grammar issues as they arise.

When students find themselves with a grammar problem, they have several options. They can seek to solve the problem themselves, with the aid of a dictionary or computer tools such as spell-check or grammar-check. They may ask someone in their group, either in their native language or in English. Or, they may seek Slater's help. When, in reading *Gulliver's Travels,* Manuel did not understand the meaning of "handkerchief," Maria, who was reading aloud with him, looked it up in a dictionary and then explained it to Manuel in Spanish.

Slater has several strategies in helping to scaffold students' learning. She may explain the issue in the group, where others, too, may listen to the discussion. Or she may ask the student to make an appointment for an individual conference in her office. For example, one afternoon, Nikolas needed some grammar help with one of his essays. The following field notes briefly describe Slater's on-the-spot lesson:

> 2:15—the class has left, Slater gives Nikolas a minilesson. She explains what an opening or topic sentence is, and why it's important, and that it's missing from his essay. She talks about the patterns (which is also the theme of the piece) of his grammar mistakes.

In this way, Slater acts in accordance with her philosophy: (a) she believes that Nikolas is ready to hear her suggestions, and (b) she looks at patterns of mistakes, not isolated ones. She has him read a problematic section aloud. When he does, he automatically corrects his mistakes; she points this out to him. She says that if he reads his work aloud to himself, he might "hear" the problems that he didn't "see." Also, when he reads aloud, he pauses appropriately where commas and periods should be. She points this out to him as well. She ties this into the theme of Visibility/Invisibility: "What you see isn't always what you think you see. When we read aloud, we interject the right thing into what we've written." Another pattern she shows him is that he drops *s*'s, so she teaches him agreement of subject and verb. Of course, one-on-one minilessons such as this take up time, and it is next to impossible to deal with every student in such detail each time.

Slater knows that mechanics and grammar are important elements of written and spoken English, but they are not the overwhelming focus of the classroom. Instead, Slater focuses on encouraging her students to think and take risks with language, to try to use new words. Grammar and the conventions of English are important and are attended to, but not as a big isolated lesson. Students themselves learn to begin solving their own language problems. Slater makes the explicit comparison between "osmosis" and learning language, saying that the brain is soaking up language all of the time. She says to the class, "One of the best ways of getting the structure of the English language into your head is reading." She goes on to tell the class that when they are reading, they are picking up punctuation, grammar, irregular verbs, and spelling. High-interest literature has great potential for engaging readers. A rich diet of reading will aid students in vocabulary development, spelling, grammar, and usage (Elley, 1997).

Reading

The broader topic of "reading" is used here instead of "literature," because students spend so much time reading other students' work. Other students' writing itself further prods student thinking, provides wonderful writing models, and generates further conversations. Multilayering at work again.

Slater's students are required to read a great deal. First, they must read a short story or chapter of a novel for their weekly literature letters. Second, Slater chooses high-interest pieces of literature for study within each topic. Students actually do read; they read constantly and clearly enjoy the literature available.

The cupboards in Slater's small classroom are filled with high-interest short stories, novels by famous authors, and magazines—in both English and other languages. She collects and buys these on her own time: "I never use textbooks, I use real books." While Slater holds all students in her class to the same general curriculum, she tries to invite novice English learners in by offering multiple versions of the same story: the original version, a simplified version, a comic book version, or an audiocassette version. With so many versions of a story to choose from, all students can read the story and get at the plot and basic ideas, discuss questions together, and collaborate in working through their activity guide. Too often, novice English learners are excluded from reading until they have mastered English language skills. Here they are expected to read and make meaning of literature.

Slater recognizes that choice plays a powerful role in learning, and so students are able to choose their own stories for their literature letters. Choices can also be made when groups work through topics for two or three weeks. For example, for the topic "Patterns and Images" students could choose to read James Thurber's "The Unicorn in the Garden," Robert Frost's "The Road Not Taken," Lewis Carroll's "Jabberwocky," Edwin Robinson's "Richard Cory," an adapted version of *Cyrano de Bergerac*, or a biography of and movie about the "Elephant Man,"—or they could focus on the art of M. C. Escher. (The range and quality of this list are typical of the kind of selections Slater offers for all topics.) Slater was particularly impressed with the way students developed empathy with the characters in the literature for this topic. In the space of three weeks, students were able to read several of the selections. Some groups read more than others, and each group chose what interested them.

Slater's book cupboards also contain literature of many different cultures to reflect the backgrounds of her students. She admits, though, that she looks for a lot of American authors for the kind of literature that will teach students the cultural perspectives of Americans. She is keen to expand their point of view. Slater explicitly tells students that reading helps them develop their English language skills and helps them learn about other people.

Slater encourages students to make use of the LaGuardia Community College library for stories to read, research information, and newspapers. She also encourages the students to use the Donnell Library in New York City, which has a large collection of young adult books and books in other languages, lots of items on tape, and a large multimedia center that lends out audio and video recordings. She has even taken groups of students there.

While Slater expects students to read at home in order to allow time for discussion in class, it was clear that students had developed their own strategies for getting into and through the reading of literature, all making use of their groups during class time. Maria and Manuel worked as a pair, reading *Gulliver's Travels* aloud and discussing vocabulary and meanings when they arose. Nina, a novice, relied on Natalie's line-by-line Spanish translation of *Gulliver's Travels*. The social context of this class allows for students to find their own way into reading. Slater does not stand in front of the class and read the story or poem aloud to students. Each group must read for themselves.

A lively literary community develops in Slater's classroom. The environment invites discussion, speculation, drawing on personal experiences, and reading. Students have real conversations on aspects of the literature that intrigue them. Clearly, these students enjoy reading.

Thinking

Slater constantly encourages her students to think more deeply about their reading, their writing, their discussions. She scaffolds and supports students' thinking in group discussion, in the activity guides, in topic essays, and in grade conferences. The three Rs ever present in her classroom seem to be *rethink, redo,* and *reflect.* Through the mastery questions in the activity guides, students are pushed to explore the philosophical and conceptual aspects of literature. These same ideas are revisited again and again in the group, and later, in connecting threads across the disciplines. Even later, when preparing graduation portfolios in their senior year, students rework selected writings from their earlier years. Both Slater and the school principal mentioned that this year the senior students expressed how much they enjoyed revisiting work from their earlier years at the school.

Slater is aware of students' zones of proximal development (Vygotsky, 1978) and is ready to push them into more difficult territory. She stretches them in their language development, in making interdisciplinary connections, and in thinking about their own learning.

Assessment

It is essential to bear in mind that Slater's teaching team is an interdisciplinary team in deed as well as in name. The students study the same themes simultaneously in all their subjects in order to deepen links among the disciplines and to learn in greater depth. In addition, much of their assessment is based on essays and projects designed to integrate the content areas through the topics and subtopics. The assessment procedures described below are a teamwide effort.

The Motion team is unique at International in that it requires two portfolios each semester: a midcycle portfolio and a final portfolio. The midcycle portfolio is designed to prepare students for their final portfolios at the end of the semester. Through the portfolios, students demonstrate their mastery of the material covered and communicate their progress to their parents. Midcycle portfolios include:

1. A summary document that catalogues their attendance, lateness, and grades, and includes assessment by themselves, their peers, and a faculty member. Students are required to include reaction sheets from two peers and one instructor.

2. A mastery essay (pulling together all three topics studied in the first half of the semester: light, macroscopic/microscopic, and images).

3. A personal statement in which students are asked to comment on their cognitive growth, personal growth, and language growth.

4. One of the three topic projects they have done, on a computer disk.

5. A letter to their parents, in their native language and in English, in which students describe what they are learning, their portfolio, their progress, and their goals. (Parents are expected to write a response to the portfolio, and their children must translate the response into English.)

Grade conferences are attended by the student and two teachers from the team. It is a forum for discussion on the students' learning and is used to set goals for the rest of the semester. Despite the Herculean task of reviewing portfolios twice a semester, the team is convinced that the midcycle portfolio is an important way for students to prepare for final portfolios.

The final portfolio develops on a much larger scale. At a minimum, it includes:

1. a cover sheet listing completed work and grades,

2. midcycle letters to and from the family,

3. all final topic essays (revised and typed),

4. a mastery essay, and

5. a personal statement.

Students choose two teachers and two peers to review and comment on their portfolio. The grade conference includes these individuals as well as two or three more peers. They sit around a table discussing portfolios one by one. Again, metacognition plays an important part in the literacy development of these students. Because the teaching team listens to students say what was difficult, they have the chance to reconsider ways to restructure during the next semester. This process also helps the team keep close tabs on students and understand them more intimately. The grade conference conversation often begins with a teacher saying, "Tell us something you did this semester that you are proud of." Students respond and then peers give feedback based on their reading of the portfolio of work. Finally, the students negotiate their grades with teachers and peers. In Slater's team, the grades were distributed across a range; they were not inflated. About 75 to 90 percent of the students passed each semester. Students learned to become self-evaluative, as demonstrated by the grades they recommended for themselves and their classmates and by the evidence they provided to support their recommendations.

Three Significant Elements of Slater's English Classroom

Students in Slater's classroom live in a rich language environment that provides a stark contrast to the traditional ESL classroom. Three important elements stand out in Slater's classroom: how the school and its teachers see their ESL learners; how Slater defines her role as teacher; and how students are prepared academically to succeed.

First, students are treated as intelligent and capable learners and are given a rigorous curriculum. A "can-do" attitude permeates this exemplary classroom. Students are immersed in language, getting the whole feel and taste of language on a daily basis. Most important, students are given dignity—they are treated as intelligent individuals, and their native language is welcomed and validated. They feel cared for in this community, which counters potential feelings of isolation and being different.

Second, Slater slowly and carefully—almost invisibly—builds a social context that both embraces the novice and pushes the more experienced language learner to more difficult territory. She has a strong philosophical understanding of learning, and so can help in nurturing language learning for her students. She has a very firm foundation in understanding what the writing process, talking-to-learn, negotiating the curriculum, and learning across the curriculum involve. She knows what she's doing but sees herself as a learner too, being flexible and open to change, knowing that no two classrooms will ever be the same. Slater exudes a "warm, colloquial flexibility" (Barnes, 1976). She clearly loves her students, and treats them with warmth and respect.

Third, it is amazing to see how these ESL students rise from their initial inexperience with the English language to developing an academic voice. Students earn their *academic clothing* throughout their time at International. They learn particular ways of talk appropriate to particular situations, whether in group work or portfolio presentations. Students explain their thinking in their own words. Interactive discourse promotes not only the learning of language but also the thoughtful learning of content. Students learn how to write and read many different genres, and they make incredible progress in their writing and reading abilities. Most important, they learn how to think about literature and nonfiction, to connect ideas across the disciplines, and to reflect on their own learning. They have opportunities not only to read and hear other students' writing and ideas, but also to learn ways of constructively giving input, challenging, and helping other students move ahead. They learn the sanctioned American way of sounding confident, a skill that will help both inside and outside of school. Their focus in classroom work is on ideas and meaning, not on piecemeal skills. As a result, they receive good preparation for future success in both academic and nonacademic endeavors.

Links between Slater's Professional Life and Her Classroom Practice

How might Slater's professional life influence the ways she teaches English and her selection of approaches to help her students achieve such great gains in their language abilities? Three influences in particular stand out: the knowledge she has gained about learning theory; the collaborative environment of International; and her focus, shared with the school overall, on reflection.

Slater's desire to understand more about how people learn led her to several pivotal professional experiences. She cites in particular the transforming effect that her yearlong participation in the New York City Writing Project had on her approach to teaching and on her understanding of the importance of the writing process. Her postgraduate study helped feed her hunger for theory and her commitment to put what she was learning into practice. What she learned from these experiences has shaped what and how she teaches English.

In addition, the focus on collaborative learning is one of the remarkable aspects of Slater's, indeed of all of International's, classes.

What must be noted is that Slater herself works in the same kind of heterogeneous, collaborative small groups that she expects her students to work in. At the team level, teachers collaboratively decide on curriculum, goals, and schedules. They also work together to find ways to help students resolve academic or personal problems, meeting collectively with the student and/or parent. Within the school, teachers in other collaborative groups handle schoolwide issues—staff development, curriculum, personnel, and special reform projects such as developing rubrics. Still wider afield, the school's professional links with LaGuardia Community College and the Partnership Schools allow for and demand further collaboration. As teachers work on these collaborative teams, they are living examples of how groups can work together and succeed. Thus, teachers are in an outstanding position to support and scaffold students' endeavors to create collaborative teams that further their individual learning and progress.

Finally, Slater is reflecting constantly on her teaching, just as she requires students to reflect constantly on their learning. As part of her professional community at International, Slater prepares portfolios, participates in peer evaluation presentations, and contributes ideas to the yearly school evaluation and goal-setting process. Slater and her colleagues at International feel that reflection is an integral part of learning, and so they make sure that teachers have built-in opportunities to reflect on their work as individuals, as team members, and as part of the school, and that students have built-in opportunities to reflect on their work as individuals and as group members. Because Slater experiences this kind of reflection process, she knows why it is important for her students to experience it and how to best provide this kind of experience for them. The entire school forms a community of learners who are prepared to take risks and try new things, and then reflect on and evaluate the outcomes collectively. Clearly, International is a place designed to bring out excellence in both teachers and students.

6 Rich Webs of Professional Support in a Suburban District

Eija Rougle
The National Research Center on English Learning
& Achievement

Cathy Starr teaches seventh-grade language arts in a school and district known for excellence in English language arts instruction. The six features of teachers' professional lives described in Chapter 3 are in evidence at Hudson Middle School on a day-to-day basis. Students are engaged in meaningful language activities, and they score higher on standardized tests in English language arts than do students in districts in similar localities with similar student populations. This chapter helps us understand why. It provides a portrait of the kind of rich professional environment that Starr both works in and creates for herself, and the effective ways in which she uses her growing knowledge of teaching language arts to enrich her students' learning as well as her own professional life.

All names in this chapter (including "Hudson Middle School" and the locality name "Schoonhavn") are pseudonyms.

The School and Its Community

The suburban community of Schoonhavn, New York, where Cathy Starr has been teaching language arts for almost thirty years, has a long-standing reputation for providing successful education. Schoonhavn is a stable, middle-class community whose population consists mostly of White, professional families whose breadwinners commute to work in neighboring cities.

People often move to Schoonhavn because of its excellent schools. Since 1990, student enrollment has climbed steadily, increasing by 20 percent. The total district enrollment in the 1995–96 academic year was 5,330 students. The district consists of five elementary schools (K–5), the Henry O. Hudson Middle School (6–8), and a high school.

Encouraging partnerships between community members and the Schoonhavn schools is a district priority. Indeed, the schools seem to play an important role in the life of the community.

The school district has a long tradition of visionary leaders. Two in particular are mentioned quite frequently by Starr: Hope Anderson and Kim Lehrer. At the time of this study (1996–1998), these two women were the driving forces in the area of professional development and curriculum planning in the district and in the middle school. Anderson, the assistant superintendent responsible for instruction and staff development, served in the district for more than two decades until she was named head of a national professional organization. Kim Lehrer, supervisor of language arts, reading, and social studies at Hudson Middle School, has been an inspiring and supportive link between the district and the middle school staff for over twenty years.

The town of Schoonhavn is near the state capital, and this proximity, along with the district's record of success, has helped to facilitate and sustain collaboration between Schoonhavn teachers and the state education department. Schoonhavn administrators and teachers have frequently been invited to participate in the formulation of educational standards for the state and share their expertise as teachers of language arts.

Hudson, Schoonhavn's one middle school, sits among green fields and community gardens at the edge of some woods. Student-made hay statues flank the flagpole near the main entrance. Inside the two-story brick building, visitors are greeted with a large "Welcome" sign and with warm smiles from both students and staff members. The walls and showcases celebrate student work of all kinds (e.g., volunteering in a soup kitchen, conserving a butterfly habitat), and "a yellow brick road" made of 3-by-5-inch index cards summarizing students' and teachers' favorite books connects all classrooms in the school to the library. Students carrying stacks of books, binders, and folders in their arms transfer peacefully from one classroom to another. No bells are heard marking the periods. Student announcers begin and end the day via an internal TV broadcast. The school gives a feeling of a bustling, positive, and orderly learning community.

Hudson's student population is ethnically, linguistically, and socioeconomically homogenous. Over 90 percent of the students are White, 0.5 percent are classified as limited-English-proficient, and 3.6 percent are eligible for free or reduced lunch (compared to 37 percent statewide). However, mainstreaming has added a level of diversity to Hudson's classrooms, for special education and physically challenged students are part of every class (specific aides are often assigned to these students).

Hudson students perform better than students in comparable statewide public schools in all academic performance tests. As an example, in 1996–97, 99 percent of Hudson's sixth graders performed above the state reference point on the reading section of the state assessment (the Pupil Evaluation Program, or PEP test). This compares to 95 percent of sixth graders in the county and 86 percent statewide. In addition, 84.4 percent of Hudson's sixth graders performed "with distinction," in comparison to 71.9 percent within the county and 53.2 percent within the state. In 1997, on the eighth-grade assessment (the Program Competency Test, PCT), 97 percent of Hudson's students performed above the state reference point in reading and 99 percent in writing. The high school graduation rate is 97 percent, and the rate of students going on to institutions of higher education is 90 percent. The student-teacher ratio is approximately thirteen to one. Of the ninety-two full-time classroom teachers at Hudson, 80 percent have earned a degree beyond the bachelor's degree.

Though Hudson serves more than twelve hundred students in grades 6 through 8, they aren't overwhelmed by the large size. The school building was designed to give the feeling of a small school. Students are assigned to one of three rectangular "houses," where they attend all their academic classes. Each house is connected to a large round building that holds the cafetorium and spaces for noisier activities such as music and art classrooms, a TV studio, a computer center, and offices. The carpeted corridors connecting the houses to the main round building form two inner courtyards. During this study, a butterfly house was being built in one of these courtyards. The school's two gyms are attached to the back side of the houses. Each house features a faculty room with desks grouped together in fours. There is also a large staff lounge with couches, round tables, and coffee and soft drink machines.

Both teachers and students are grouped into grade-level-specific teams. For example, Starr is part of an interdisciplinary team of four seventh-grade teachers (language arts, social studies, science, and math) that is responsible for teaching approximately 110 seventh graders in the "Totem House." The teacher team assigns these 110 students into four heterogeneous classes, and they regroup these classes after each ten-week marking period. Thus Starr teaches language arts to four classes of seventh graders who are all on the same team. The purpose for this team approach is explained in a school document:

The purpose of teaming at Henry O. Hudson Middle School is to provide a structure that will promote, to the greatest degree possible, academic success for every student in the school. Through teaming, the school is able to allow small groups of teachers to work with a portion of the student body. These teaching teams are able to use their shared teaching expertise, daily opportunities for team planning, and extra contact time, as well as working with colleagues and parents or using in-house and community resources to meet the needs of their students. The team structure provides the flexibility, creativity, and organization to meet student's individual needs. The structure is designed so that students can be known well and feel a sense of belonging and connection. Teams are expected to collaborate and help each other to bring about student success and, in the process, support each other's growth and learning.

The teacher teams meet daily and have shared planning time. Usually all four of the teachers are present at parent conferences, as are the assigned student counselors. Teachers also meet in disciplinary grade-level-specific teams (e.g., Starr meets with all the seventh-grade language arts teachers). Thus the practical work rests on two "horizontal" teams: the interdisciplinary team and the disciplinary team. In department meetings (which sometimes combine social studies and language arts), teachers in the same discipline meet across the grades (e.g., sixth-, seventh-, and eighth-grade language arts teachers). This organizational structure allows for many contexts in which teachers can interact with each other professionally.

Hudson also offers an extensive variety of other activities and support programs. For example, teachers are available during one period a day specifically for tutoring. Thus the tutoring is integrated with daily instruction. In addition, the school offers "Strive for Success," an evening activity in which parents come to school to work with their children on study skills. Another offering, "Seven to Eight Team," is designed to help at-risk students with their academic skills and with issues of trust; in this program, twelve seventh graders and twelve eighth graders receive individual attention each day from a school counselor. For enrichment, the school offers activities open to everyone, such as a debate group, a math olympiad, a law club, a history group, and a mythology club, which meet before school begins in the morning.

In line with the district priority to invite "parents, staff, and other community members to explore, understand, and participate in ways that support learning for all," Hudson encourages community links and parental involvement. The eighteen-member school "cabinet," which makes schoolwide decisions, includes three parents. The brochure "Get to Know Your School" outlines over a dozen different types of parent volunteer opportunities. Parents are invited, for instance, to assist students with research, to read to them, and to help in the learning and computer centers. Hudson's community resource coordinator matches parents' interests with students' needs. The school also offers activities designed to include parents, such as a family evening at a local ice hockey stadium that Starr's team planned.

Community links are varied. For example, as part of a U.S. Department of Education Goals 2000 grant, the district partnered with a local writer's institute to organize a discussion on evolutional biology at the nearby university. Students were able to discuss issues with and ask questions of the well-known scientist, author, and professor Stephen Jay Gould. During Hudson's "Disability Month," the school invited many speakers from the community to give presentations at the school, including one of Starr's former students, who is blind. Students are also encouraged to volunteer in the community. They may help senior citizens in nursing homes, assist with reading programs in libraries, or work with after-school programs in the community center.

"Recognition Breakfasts" honor and congratulate students for their performances. Teachers nominate students, and approximately forty are chosen, based on merits of achievement, steady improvement and effort, and supportiveness to fellow students.

The following words in a Schoonhavn brochure seem to summarize the environment of the Schoonhavn school community: "At Schoonhavn, every student is important, every staff member is part of the educational team, every parent is treated as a key player, and every community member is welcome in our schools."

Starr's Professional Life

Starr is a veteran teacher with a bachelor's degree in English education and a master's degree in reading. After teaching for about fifteen years, she returned to school to earn the advanced degree. Most of her career has involved teaching middle school students in Schoonhavn. However, she started teaching more than thirty years ago on Long Island. There, she explains, administrators handed down the curriculum and assessments to teachers, allowing no opportunities for input. In fact, she was simply given "a course outline based on following the [assigned] grammar and literature books." In Schoonhavn, she found quite a different view of the teacher's role:

> When I arrived in Schoonhavn, I was surprised to find teachers designing programs and selecting tests and paperbacks. That was new to me, but not to teachers in Schoonhavn. This expectation of participation and input was fostered by a strong inservice program and supported by opportunities to attend workshops and conferences.

At Schoonhavn, this "expectation of participation and input" is fostered on every level, from curriculum development to district-sponsored activities to department meetings to classroom learning. It is a top priority at Schoonhavn to provide the time, opportunities, and kind of environment that encourage teachers to share their thoughts and ideas, learn from each other, expose themselves to new approaches and processes, contribute their experiences, and reflect on their own practice. Anderson, the assistant superintendent responsible for instruction and staff development, explained in an interview: "You have to create the situations that allow for the thinking to happen, [and] not only create the situations, but the climate—that [input] is expected, that your ideas are going to be seriously considered."

Anderson let teachers know that "We can't do without your mind. We need everybody's mind." In fact, when asked about her goals for language arts, Anderson explained that she worked *with* teams to develop agreed-upon goals and that she feels it is very important that goals be developed in a collaborative way. She added, "My ideas become stronger as I hear others think, and it also helps me to clarify my ideas." As a result, "We begin to really say what we mean as we question one another."

The opportunities for such professional discourse and interaction abound at Schoonhavn. "How could you possibly even describe all the interactions that go on here?" says Starr, as she tries to explain this invaluable aspect of her professional life:

> The interaction with colleagues in this building is a total part of whoever I am. It's such a different experience from when I taught on Long Island. It's not fair to compare because I'm sure it's different today, but . . . [then] you came in, you did your job, and you went home. You may have said hello or [had] lunch with some people, but you didn't really do an awful lot of professional sharing. There's a lot of professional conversation that goes on here every day. Some of it is planned; some of it is informal.

Interdisciplinary Teams

Starr meets with the three other teachers on her team (science, social studies, and math) every morning at 9:00. They gather in the team's faculty room around the four teacher desks to plan together and to discuss how to support the students they serve. The stated purposes of these daily team meetings are to:

- identify learning results for students on the team and plan how to achieve them;
- integrate curriculum and share instructional strategies that develop student learning and meet the learning needs of individual students;
- organize and schedule the instructional program within their team;
- consult with teachers who are not team members but who teach the same group of students (e.g., art, music, home and careers, and technology education);
- develop a positive, respecting learning community for the members of the team;
- hold case conferences on specific students;
- share strategies that meet the needs of the diversity of students on the team;
- plan ways to help students develop study skills;
- develop research goals.

As an example, during one team meeting I observed, the four teachers were discussing an interdisciplinary unit on Mayan culture and symbol systems. As they shared ideas about how to best proceed with the unit, the science teacher suggested that students should take notes and underline while reading the text. Starr shared her understanding of thoughtful reading by adding: "I tell [the students] when they underline: 'Put in the margin why. Explain, at least give a reason.' [This] encourages . . . good strategies with note taking."

Language Arts Colleagues at Hudson

Starr's interactions with language arts teachers at Hudson are truly an integral part of her day. As she chronicled in her log during one typical day, she chatted with eight different colleagues at various times. Some of the discussions dealt with students, some were about sharing material, or a personal memory, or an impression of a book. Sometimes when there is a need (and time available), the seventh-grade language arts teachers meet. Starr called these meetings "a gift," alluding to the value that teachers place on the time they can spend discussing discipline-related issues. This group of seventh-grade language arts teachers is a supportive network. Starr refers to them as colleagues but also as "friends, neighbors, car-pool buddies, and roommates during conferences." As she wrote in her log:

> Ordinarily we schedule occasional meetings as we please, usually at 8:00 A.M. These are not required; they are our meetings, scheduled by us when we feel the need. . . . I was trying to decide why this meeting seemed ordinary to me. Perhaps it's because we exchange ideas continuously in informal ways, and we don't require meetings or outside influences to do that. . . . We will talk about something we are doing. Often it is that spontaneous sharing of excitement over a successful lesson or unit. We exchange papers, new ideas, etc.

Other types of informal meetings include "a coffee group" that gets together daily and a book club that meets several times a year. All of these contacts build care and concern among the staff.

Once a month there is also a contractual hour-long meeting from 3:30 to 4:30. This hour is often used for department meetings, although if there is a need for an all-staff or all-house meeting, that will occur instead. According to Starr, "the department is another place where there's a lot of support." Lehrer, the language arts department head, sets the tone for department meetings. She uses this time when the teachers come together as a way to support professional development. As she explains:

> My primary goal is to help people move forward as individuals . . . [and] as a department—to be sure that we're sharing a vision, that we are involved very actively in what's going on in our field. I guess [I'm] more than a facilitator, sometimes an agitator.

Lehrer sees department meetings as opportunities for thinking and for helping teachers stretch their knowledge. For example, she says, "My goal is for everyone to leave at the end of a meeting, which is the last hour of the day (4:30), energized and wanting to learn more, think more about something that we've talked about."

During one department meeting, for example, Lehrer and the teachers were discussing state-developed standards for writing and the types of writing samples to be collected in students' writing folders. The atmosphere was very thoughtful, ideas were tossed around and discussed, and questions were raised. Starr raised a concern about the genres listed on the state's guidelines, which were handed out at the meeting. "I still have a problem—something is not captured. [There is] no place to show students' personal writing. [This is] something for the cabinet to consider." In this way, Starr was reiterating part of her writing curriculum and putting on the table an important aspect of writing. Another teacher talked about the limitations of the suggested listings.

In this meeting, the intellectual dialogue about larger issues (in this case, genres of writing) was privileged because it was given all the meeting time, whereas no time was spent on the other item on the agenda, which dealt with the onus of reporting how and when conventions are being taught. This detailed information was passed out as a handout.

Later, Starr wrote in her log:

> The meeting got us thinking. We haven't really worried much about aligning with standards because we all work so hard to provide quality education. I heard people expressing concern about the initial list. No one wants to lower expectations to meet state expectations. I don't think that will happen, but I do think we will need to do a lot of talking and thinking together. We are used to that, so I don't see a problem.
>
> This was a typical language arts meeting. Everyone expresses ideas and most are heard. Even the least experienced feels free to talk. I like that.

There are times when people at Hudson have reconsidered whether or not they should continue having two sets of teams: the four-member interdisciplinary teams and the subject departments. Lehrer mentioned in an interview that some staff members have suggested that "we should eliminate the departments and just put all the energy into teams. I could never allow that to happen." She explains further:

> I think you need to balance both things. I think you need to have interdisciplinary concerns and look for connections in the world and ways to teach children that make the learning real and solid for them. But I also think, as a member of a discipline, [that] passion is a really key thing. People's passions are in different directions. I think you can derive great passion from your discipline.

Additional Collaborative Opportunities at Hudson

Starr has opportunities to work with other staff members at Hudson in collaborative ways for a variety of purposes. For example, in one year she served on two schoolwide committees; one focused on using technology, the other on relationships between teachers and administrators. In addition, department meetings are sometimes extended to include another discipline. During one such meeting, language arts teachers, science teachers, their respective supervisors, and a librarian discussed the writing that students are asked to do in science classes. Starr shared some of the rubrics she has developed to help her and her students better understand and assess writing assignments. She described the meeting in her log:

> We talked about how much writing goes on in science class. Students write lab reports, summaries, and research papers. We discussed how rubrics can help with evaluation for the teachers, and help parents and students understand expectations. We shared rubrics that are currently in use, and everyone agreed that this is a helpful practice.

Another example of the kind of professional sharing that Starr participates in at Hudson is an art workshop she attended. She not only learned a great deal during the workshop, but she was also able to share ideas with the art teacher:

> The experience was wonderful—relaxing and gratifying. But even more, I enjoyed [the art teacher's] delightful teaching style and the way she encouraged her timid, adult students. It is valuable to see what and how other subject-area teachers present and develop their curriculum.
>
> After the workshop, [the art teacher] and I started chatting. She shared how she used posters of artwork to draw out students, and I shared my experiences with transparencies [works of art on transparency film that are sometimes included with literature anthologies because they relate to the literature presented]. She uses many of the techniques I use in literature discussions in her approach to thinking about and responding to art.

Later, Starr continued this conversation with the art teacher to build further on the ideas they had begun exploring together. In this, as in most of her other professional conversations, she was always seeking to learn more about her profession.

Another way that the spirit of collaboration and sharing are used to foster professional growth is the school policy of inhouse observation. Teachers may request time off to observe a colleague's class whenever they like, for this is viewed as an important aspect of professional development.

Professional Associations

Starr is clearly a teacher whose professional activities are not confined within her classroom walls, or for that matter within the boundaries of her school. She participates very actively in the professional organizations in the field of language arts. She has written numerous journal articles (e.g., in *Language Arts* and *English Journal*). For an article in *English Journal,* she was given the Paul and Kate Farmer Writing Award by the National Council of Teachers of English (NCTE) for contributions to wider conversations in the field.

A decisive moment for Starr came in 1988 when she was invited to participate in a research collaboration exploring literature instruction with Judith Langer. She participated due to "curiosity" and "being intrigued about learning more about ways to engage students in thinking about literature." Becoming involved with the university community had an energizing impact on her. She talks about making contact with the "real people" behind the articles she'd been reading in the many journals that Anderson or Lehrer had always been pointing out. She valued "the opportunity to really sit down and talk about things . . . [with] another community." It "broadens the horizon," she explained, counteracting the tendency for teachers to become isolated in their classrooms. This opportunity to stand back, reflect on, and learn more about teaching language arts was invaluable to her, and spurred her to join NCTE. It is noteworthy that Schoonhavn has strong professional ties to NCTE; both Anderson and Lehrer have held leading positions, nationally and regionally, in NCTE. Thus they have been participating in and shaping the disciplinary discussions of the field and bringing that knowledge to Schoonhavn for a long time.

Starr was on the NCTE steering committee for the secondary level. In this role she read hundreds of conference proposals and articles. However, when asked what, in all this reading, had really stood out to her, she mentioned names of people she had actually worked with or listened to during presentations and workshops. Face-to-face interactions seem to be important, and, fortunately, Starr has experienced many of these. For example, in the spring Starr traveled out of state twice for NCTE—for a working session of the steering committee and to chair a section of a spring conference.

Starr's attendance at and participation in NCTE conferences have given her very rich material to ponder and have often left ideas percolating in the back of her mind. For example, after one conference presentation by Shirley Brice Heath, Starr noted in her log that

> her strongest point for me was that children need the arts. She emphasized that her work showed that children need three things from life: connections, tasks, and art. I need to revisit her work (maybe this summer) before I can make connections with her talk.

As Starr engages in her professional work—reading conference proposals, chairing a session, or listening to presentations—she has a sounding board, a counterpoint to reflect on what she knows about teaching and learning language arts. In a way, she is carrying on a dialogue with multiple professional voices. Her log entries bear witness to this "conversation." Even though these threads of broader and more distant conversations may stay covert inside an individual's head, they are important as seedbeds for ideas, questions, and critiques to be developed and perhaps later articulated. For example, following the NCTE spring conference, her log captures a concern: "I always worry when an idea becomes a package. What I hope all teachers will do [is] use the book as a starting point and make it fit their needs rather than seeing it as 'the way' to teach literature" (Starr log). In response to another presentation, she expresses her deeper concern:

> The audience didn't seem to be concerned that the activities distributed required the students to display almost no understanding of the books, make no comparisons between and among the cultures represented, and engage in no conversations about their understandings or questions. As I was worrying about the message going out, especially to the young people in the audience, I jotted down the following quotes from the lead presenter (make a paper airplane, origami, design a T-shirt, etc.). All of those are fun activities but cannot replace writing and discussing ideas. . . . How can these people [teacher presenters], who are well meaning, be encouraged to look more deeply at their practice? How can we help teachers move beyond projects to thinking?

Sometimes the ideas Starr encounters in these professional associations come together in a way that extends her knowledge and changes how she teaches. For example, in her work with the research project, Starr learned a great deal about using an inquiry approach to teaching literature. At first, she wasn't able to extend that approach to students' research projects, but two additional professional development activities helped her develop the ideas and impetus needed to try inquiry-based research with her students. First, she participated in a technology workshop in the school library, which initiated an ongoing conversation with other teachers and the librarian. The following summer, they participated in a districtwide three-day workshop led by an NCTE staff member. Starr worked with the presenter so that she could specifically address the interests and concerns of the participants. As a result, in the fall, for the first time, she structured a research project for her students using an inquiry approach: students researched African American contributions to society based on their own questions. As a concluding phase, Starr and the school librarian discussed the research project and then wrote a short note about the future development of inquiry-based research in a library publication. Starr's log documents the conversation with the librarian and gives evidence of assessing students' learning during the inquiry and extending her own understanding of what it means to use inquiry as a tool for learning. She structured this conversation in terms of "gains" and "losses":

> 8:00 a.m. this morning I met with [the] librarian to discuss research project completed last fall. The point was to use inquiry to get students excited about research and to really get them to search for information:
>
> We talked about gains:
>
> a. Students phrasing own questions and then rephrasing those questions when search redirected them.
> b. Students finding resources far broader than in past.
> c. Students using Internet to gain information.
> d. Students searching outside of school not only in libraries but in record and video outlets, etc.
> e. Students developing wide variety of ways to present knowledge.
>
> "Losses" (as viewed by some):
>
> a. [No] Guaranteed coverage of certain topics since students used own questions and interest.
> b. No formal writing pieces since students selected own format for sharing knowledge.
> c. [No] Control over use of research material—could not be sure every student "hit" basic reference sources.
>
> The one thing we both agreed on was that we should try this again. We need to give students more time and freedom to explore and to provide more opportunities for creative expression.

Thus in this example, Starr carried out conversations across various contexts, at various times, and with various colleagues. Starr built on and extended her professional knowledge through this web of interactions. The various layers of professional networking were instrumental in extending her knowledge and practical pedagogy about a specific concept, inquiry. It's no wonder that she characterizes her professional associations as "amazing growth opportunities."

How Language Arts Are Taught and Learned in Starr's Classroom

Cathy Starr is an energetic woman who is totally absorbed by and focused on her seventh-grade students during language arts class.

Wearing soft-soled shoes, she moves among the groups of students, scaffolding discussion or checking the thinking at the tables or reading and commenting on students' work. When stopping to talk with a student, she lifts her glasses, which have been perched on her nose, to the top of her head. Her voice carries genuine warmth and excitement. Her enthusiasm and interest are reflected by the class. A student turned to an observer in the classroom during an initial observation and announced: "Mrs. Starr is the best teacher in the world."

Her classroom is filled with books. One wall is occupied by large, metal storage shelves containing boxes with student folders, copies of literature anthologies, books on language arts scholarship (including authors such as Atwell, Langer, Probst, and Scholes). A smaller bookcase is loaded with approximately five hundred paperback novels. The teacher's desk, swelling with papers, is tucked in a corner. Posted along one wall is the text, "We read to know we are not alone."

Instead of having individual desks, students sit around tables arranged in an octagon. During presentations and whole-class discussions, students push their chairs, which have tennis ball-cushioned legs, into a circle in front of the tables. The classroom is physically arranged to facilitate interactions where students' voices are heard. Indeed, students have many opportunities to listen to, converse with, and work with each other. In fact, as they left the classroom on any given day, they were often still talking together about issues discussed in class.

The approach Hudson takes toward the teaching of language arts, as well as the skills and knowledge that should be learned at various grade levels, are described in a five-page district document developed and revised by a committee of administrators, teachers, and parents. It states:

> English language arts instruction in the Schoonhavn School District is based on the study and use of language. Language is a means of structuring and representing knowledge. As children listen, speak, read, draw, or write, they construct meaning through language. Language, by its very nature, is dynamic, full of power, meaning, and complexity. Its social nature allows students to become active language users through listening, speaking, reading, and writing. Language can empower students and play a key role in helping them become responsive, informed citizens. . . . Knowledge and use of the conventions of grammar, usage, spelling, and punctuation are critical to effective communication. In the classroom, these skills are introduced, directly

taught, modeled, and practiced within the context of meaningful language experience.

As for how the language arts fit into the interdisciplinary
approach at Hudson, assistant superintendent Anderson explained
that language arts teachers "have a responsibility to help students to be
powerful with language. Part of where you get that power is in the literary. But you also need the experience of writing about the nonliter-
ary—to use that language and power that you discovered [in language
arts classes] in situations that help you negotiate the world."

Starr appreciates the district's philosophy about teaching language arts. Her students learn about and use language in a stimulating
yet safe environment where thinking is valued and encouraged, and
listening and responding respectfully to one another are the norm. A
large part of her instruction is devoted to helping students "be able to
think and share ideas—take what other people say, maybe process
that, and weigh it and balance it against what they know and think." In
Starr's classroom, every important assignment culminates in a public
presentation through which the student not only demonstrates content
knowledge but also communicates that knowledge in a suitable format
(e.g., a formal report for research, a story for a family history). Thus,
every student is encouraged to develop oral as well as writing skills.

When, at the end of the school year, the six students I interviewed were asked to fill in a questionnaire describing what they had
learned in their English class, five students indicated that they learned
to improve their writing; several had learned to consider and appreciate different views; and some added to the list that they learned to
carry on a class discussion about books. For example, Keona wrote that
she had learned:

> 1. How to write a poem. 2. Essays. 3. Looked at art pieces the
> way we looked at stories. 4. Class discussions—different opin-
> ions. 5. Learned about each other and ourselves.

Peter wrote, "I have learned spelling, better grammar, punctuation, and word usage. I have learned to write stories better & more flu-
ently. How to understand people's ideas."

Keona's answer to a question about what she thought one
needed to learn in English was: "To read, understand poems and Art,
understand people's opinions and differences." Clearly, for these students, Starr's classroom is a place not just to study language and its
conventions, but also a place to *use* language and become better at
reading, writing, and communicating about knowledge with others. In
addition, students say they have learned to take something they know

how to do (interpret stories) and apply that knowledge in a new situation (looking at art).

So, how does Starr facilitate language arts learning? When asked what takes place in her classroom, she replies: "lots of reading, lots of writing, lots of discussion, lots of student questions."

"Lots of Reading"

According to Starr, the primary part of language arts is literature. Students in her classroom read extensively and respond to what they're reading by writing in their journals. All seventh-grade classes at Hudson read the same two full-length novels during the year. Starr's students also read and discuss numerous short stories and poems. Independently, each student reads some twenty to thirty novels and reflects on this reading by writing regularly in a journal, generating questions, and capturing his or her understanding of elements such as character and plot. Reading and writing work in tandem in Starr's classroom. She uses journal writing as an opportunity to assess and reinforce students' developing abilities to express themselves. Her written comments are supportive, encouraging, and instructive. For example, in the case of Jason, who had recently moved to the district, Starr responded to his first journal entry in this way: "Jason, when you write, try to stay focused on one idea." In response to Matt, who had written an entire page about "Rules" in one paragraph, she wrote: "You have a good idea here. You need to add some punctuation."

Starr expects students to engage actively and thoughtfully in their reading. For example, one assignment in early fall involved reading Sandra Cisneros's "Eleven," an essayistic short story about an unpleasant event in school (from *Woman Hollering Creek and Other Stories*). To help students interact mindfully with the text, Starr asked them to read with a pen and a pencil in their hands. The students read the piece twice, each time writing their comments and questions directly on the page, first with one implement and then the other. Thus, not only was thinking made overt, but the use of different colors in recording ideas revealed the added layers of student thought. Colleen circled and underlined portions of the text and then wrote her comments next to them, commenting on both content and craft. For instance, she underlined the sentence "Only today I wish I didn't have only eleven years rattling inside me like pennies in a tin Band-Aid box." She wrote "Good simile" next to it, and wrote these notes in the margin: "That makes a lot of sense. I remember that a lot." Starr's comment on the top of the page read: "Great way to respond to literature! I like your thinking! A+".

As with these examples, Starr frequently makes sure she uses her responses to scaffold students' growing ability to communicate their ideas clearly. Sometimes, however, she feels the need is simply to express care and interest. For example, when Amanda wrote in her journal about a difficult family situation, Starr showed her support by writing: "You are really being strong!" And elsewhere: "Let me know how the hayride was. You are fortunate to have so many family members nearby. I grew up in a situation like that and it was great fun."

"Lots of Writing"

At Hudson, writing is an integral part of envisioning literature (Langer, 1995). It is used as a thinking tool for students as they read novels—making predictions, asking questions, and summarizing what they have read so far. Students also learn to use strategies such as Venn diagrams and idea maps to aid them as they think through how to organize their ideas for their writing projects. Starr's students do a great deal of writing and learn to write for a variety of purposes, including getting into and thinking through an assignment, communicating ideas to others, and expressing themselves. They write in various genres, such as poetry, letters, narratives, and fairy tales. They also write for practical reasons such as keeping records and managing tasks. For example, during the inquiry research project, students reflected upon the inquiry process by writing notes in their journals about what they had done so far and what they needed to do next.

Writing projects go through several stages. Students are assisted throughout the process; for example, every writing assignment includes a conference with a peer or a teacher. All students have "Work in Progress" folders. They keep an editing sheet inside these folders to help themselves and their peer readers check the content, grammar, punctuation, and spelling of their pieces. During peer conferences, when students are reviewing their work together, they know that they need to stay focused, respectful, and thoughtful. "Our kids, to a huge extent, see themselves as writers," explained department chair Lehrer. One such student, Nick, describes in an interview his strategy for writing an assigned essay:

> I thought I did pretty good on [the essay], 'cause I got real, I explained it good, and I thought about it a lot. I made two different types of plans. That way I would get it almost perfect. Before I do the rough draft, I did a web [in which] you write your subject and different things going off on your subject. Then I did idea boxes—you just put the things that you would like to put in

your essay in a couple of categories. I figured each of those categories would be separate paragraphs, and I could work from
there. Then after that, I showed my mom. She's like the editor of
the family, and so she evaluated that. Then I typed it up on the
computer.

Students have a sense of ownership about their writing. When
Starr gives an assignment, she seldom controls the topic or form but
explicitly teaches several different genres (e.g., persuasive essay,
poem). She encourages students to use their personal experience or
understanding of an issue as a starting point. When asked to provide
topics for a persuasive essay, students suggested: a study on school
lunches, making lockers bigger, the snack bar in the cafeteria, a family
vacation, and what it is like to be a thirteen-year-old boy. For example,
Ben used one such opportunity to air his annoyance at the narrowness
of school lockers and wrote a persuasive essay to argue for roomier
storage for students. The texts written by students are usually performed and shared with an audience. Thus their pieces of writing
become literary artifacts with an expectation of audience response.

An example of very personal writing is a weeklong poetry unit
that resulted in a plethora of poems, which were then read by students
and enjoyed and responded to by listeners. As with all of the assignments in Starr's classroom, this project grew out of a shared experience
during which students learned to consider best examples of the craft
(in this case, a poem by Robert Frost). They then tried to write poems
on their own. It was an accumulative experience that built from one
lesson to another. Starr explains what she did in the poetry unit this
way:

> I . . . read this poem one day and said, "What bothers you? What
> don't you understand?" And then the second day I said, "What
> questions do you have? What do you think it means?"
> [The n]ext day [we] listened to the sounds, and the next day we
> talked a little bit about the vocabulary. We talked about rhyme
> scheme and sounds.

In addition to listening to poetry and considering the literary
devices of the genre, students were engaged in looking at pictures of
paintings as well. As I described earlier, Starr had participated in a
workshop given by the school's art teacher. Starr then talked further
with the art teacher to explore how she could use art to help her students experience and create their own literature. Starr decided to try
connecting the interpretation of a painting with writing poetry. During
her unit on poetry, therefore, she included some lessons in which she

led a discussion about individual paintings, the feelings they evoked, and how they can help viewers construct meaning and then interpret art through poetry. For her students this meant a whole new kind of learning and stretching, as evidenced by their end-of-the-year comments reported above. As an example of the kind of learning that occurred, here is a poem that Ted wrote after studying the painting "Wake of the Ferry II" (John Sloan, 1907):

> It's bleak, it's bleak
> What is the mystique
> He stands alone.
> It's bleak, it's bleak, where floor boards creak,
> He stands alone.
> It's bleak, it's bleak, where most are meek,
> He stands alone.
> It's bleak, it's bleak where most are weak,
> He stands alone, he stands alone.

He explains his thoughts as he was crafting the poem:

> Dreary day, and like, someone, some lonely person or something like that, just standing there or looking out at something. I just tried to, like I looked at the picture and saw that it was dreary and it would be hard to rhyme stuff with dreary, so I felt like I was in the mood for a rhyming poem you know. And, so since that was kind of hard to rhyme enough with dreary, so I decided to go with bleak, since that was my second word that I had in my mind, and I found four good words that fit the poem, that rhymed with bleak, and so I worked around that, and kind of made it a repeat, a repetitive poem, except a couple of words changed, like we've seen examples of it in the book, and I kind of like that style, and so I decided to do it like that. . . . I made three drafts. . . . I molded it pretty good, so to speak.

For the most part, grammar is taught within the context of students' writing. Especially at the beginning of the year, Starr gives daily minilessons on grammar, with related worksheets. But most of the grammar instruction comes from her corrections and comments on students' writing assignments. It is within this context that she focuses on punctuation, spelling, literary terms, and usage. Vocabulary development, too, comes in context—for example, numerical prefixes in a unit on Mayan culture and symbol systems, or etymology while researching students' family names. In addition, Starr displays posters of grammar rules (e.g., *it's* versus *its*) throughout the room so that students can use them for reference when writing and editing. Her approach to teaching grammar aligns with the state language arts frameworks, quoted in Schoonhavn's "Language Arts Expectations":

Skills are taught when students' work and/or performance indicates a need for them. Teachers understand that skills are acquired through experience and development, as well as through direct instruction and demonstration. The emphasis is on learning language within a context of purposeful language use.

"Lots of Discussion, Lots of Student Questions"

Students have numerous opportunities to share their ideas with each other through whole-class and small-group discussions, as well as in responding to each other's writing. For example, Amanda wrote that what she liked best about language arts class was "working with other people, because I get to learn new ways of looking at things, and I like being able to make a say in what we do." Clearly there is a climate of respect, openness, and participation that helps facilitate such interaction. Starr's interactions with and comments to students serve as an excellent model for students as they learn how to establish and maintain this valued climate.

Starr encourages participation to such an extent that she invited parents to participate in literature discussions on Lois Lowry's book *The Giver*. The book engages contemporary issues and controversies, and Starr thought it would provide an opportunity for parents to have some input into what went on in her classroom. And indeed, many parents participated in whole-class literature discussions on *The Giver*.

An example of the central role that student-to-student discussion and student participation play in Starr's classroom can be seen in the final exam that she assigned for her class. This culminating activity lasted for two weeks and required students to work both within a group and individually. The assignment was as follows.

Task: You will select a short story to study. At the end of your study, you will prepare a presentation for the class that will share your learning.

Expectations:

Group
1. Choose a story from the list that everyone agrees to read.
2. Develop a plan for reading.
3. Complete required group assignments (discussion).
4. Prepare a presentation for the class.
5. Assign responsibilities to each member of the group.
6. Be considerate of other groups' efforts.

Individual

1. Read the story according to schedule developed by the group.
2. Participate in group discussions and activities.
3. Complete individual assignments.
4. Actively participate in group presentations.
5. Be considerate of other students' needs.

Requirements:

Group

1. Develop a calendar for reading and discussion.
2. Hold at least one group discussion. Complete a note sheet for each discussion.
3. Complete at least one written conversation in pairs or triads.
4. Have group members share journal entries at least once.
5. Research information about the author of your story. (optional)
6. Maintain all record sheets in group folder.
7. Prepare a script for the group presentation.

Individual

1. Write at least one journal entry about this story. Use the techniques we have used when reading novels and short stories during the school year. You may include sketches in your entries.
2. Respond to entries of other group members.
3. Complete all tasks assigned by group.

Starr wanted to extend her students' readings and learning, even on the final exam. She had her students choose from a list of short stories they had not read before, and, in order to complete this culminating assignment, they would need to thoughtfully apply skills and strategies they had learned throughout the year.

This exam shows the key role that Starr assigns to the process of students' learning from each other. Students are expected to articulate their (momentary) understandings of the short story to each other in their small groups and then, through discussion and individual and group writing, present the group's collective understanding of the text. Students were very thoughtful in their responses to each others' ideas. For example, in response to one student's journal entry, another student wrote: "I think that your response is just like mine except that you needed to have a better choice of words. I agree that Jo and her brother had a normal relationship." Another student wrote: "Although I disagree with your opinions, you wrote this entry pretty well." And Nick had this response attached to his entry: "In reading Nick's response to the story 'Rip van Winkle' it seemed to me that Nick was confused about what was going on because [of] all the questions he would have liked to ask Mr. Irving. To me though, if Nick had all the questions he asked answered, he might have enjoyed the book more. Sincerely, Patrick."

As can be seen, students offered helpful comments to their peers in a thoughtful and respectful way. They seemed to learn a great deal from each other in this kind of context, as Daniel showed in this comment on his end-of-year questionnaire: "Right now we are taking a final exam and it is teaching me how to work better in a group. I think that it is kind of fun and a good thing to do. It helps me focus better and get to know the story better."

The example of Starr's final exam shows how she helps students learn to use language as a purposeful tool. It also emphasizes that learning is supported by participation in a group. And finally, the teaching and learning of English in her classroom is always geared toward the future. Even the final examination is a learning experience.

Assessment

Three characteristics stand out regarding Starr's approach to assessing her students' work. First, assessment is closely woven into instruction; it is built in as a thread running through the assignments. Second, she is flexible in designing assessments, allowing them to evolve as needed. Third, her assessments focus on students' strengths.

One of the primary ways that Starr integrates assessment into instruction is through rubrics. She develops rubrics for each assignment. She also has general rubrics that students can use as they are editing, revising, and assessing their own or a peer's writing. Each rubric includes a self-assessment component so that students are constantly required to assess their own learning and performance. She explains that her rubrics serve many purposes:

> Early in the year I use [rubrics] so that the students know the expectations for the assignment. The parents like having it as well. It helps them focus on areas for improvement as they assist with the work. It is a tremendous help to me as I grade assignments. . . . I think I can be more objective when it is clear to me *what* I expect. Then, as the students become more familiar with

the rubric, they can get a better sense of *how* well they have met expectations in addition to *what* those expectations are.

She also ties assessment to instruction when she grades student writing. She writes comments directly on the pages of students' journals, as shown above, and also grades for effort and completeness. For note taking while reading a story, she gives credit for "asking good questions and showing thinking and engagement." In order to push reluctant students to use journals to reflect on their own effort during an inquiry project, Starr decided she needed to read and assess each student's writing more frequently. In fact, she graded each journal entry "to get them to evaluate the experience" and to help students develop a habit of reflective writing, since students would be using the journals to record their thoughts while reading novels later in the year. By putting a great deal of focus on commenting on and evaluating student journal entries, Starr is using this kind of ongoing assessment as an instructional tool.

Second, Starr lets the form of her assessments, specifically the final exam, evolve over a period of time. At Hudson, language arts teachers and interdisciplinary teams have much leeway in designing their individual final exams, which tend to take the form of a five-day writing exam.

Starr thinks about the final exam throughout the year, taking into consideration situational needs and where students are in their learning. By November, she had noted that "many of her students [this year] will need a more structured approach" for the final exam than last year's class, which prepared learning portfolios.

Third, for Starr, assessment is a means of finding out and showing what students are able to do rather than what their shortcomings are. She uses assessment to focus on students' strengths. In addition to the many oral and written presentations students are required to do during the year, she also encourages students to express themselves in other forms, including illustrations, photographs, videotapes, music, and sculpture. For example, because the social studies and science classes included writing components in their final exams last year, Starr decided not to have students do more writing for the language arts exam. She wrote in her journal that January: "I would also like to give kids who are not strong writers an opportunity to bloom and prove themselves in other forms." She finally decided to have students reflect on their most meaningful learning experiences inside and outside of school and to prepare a "learning portfolio" to present to two readers and the class. The assignment was a very well crafted and powerful tool for self-reflection and it also became an important link between the child, the learner, and the home.

The Relationship between Starr's Professional Life and the Way Language Arts Is Taught and Learned in Her Classroom

Hudson Middle School's philosophy statement emphasizes that "all members of the school community are continually involved in the active process of learning." As a member of the Schoonhavn Central District community and as a teacher at Hudson Middle School, Starr is able to partake in a very rich professional life. The learning experiences available to her as a Schoonhavn teacher—the various participatory meetings, workshops, and networking opportunities, and the involvement in virtually every level of school activity (goal setting, planning, decision making, curriculum development)—are effective. And they model, in many ways, the kind of effective learning experiences available to her language arts students. For example, the district and the school have an "expectation of participation and input." Assistant Superintendent Anderson doesn't make goals without involving teachers. Hudson language arts supervisor Lehrer encourages teachers to think through and share their thoughts about how the department should handle issues such as state writing standards. Teachers are willing to participate because they feel respected and supported. In addition, teachers are given the time and forum to discuss issues and work together.

One could draw parallels with Starr's language arts class. Students are encouraged to participate and to feel a sense of ownership about their writing and learning, often choosing the topic, approach, or form of their work. They feel respected and cared for when they see their teacher's responses to their journals and other writing assignments. Students are also given ample opportunities to discuss with and learn from their peers during their many whole-class and small-group discussions and their group assignments and exams. In short, Starr treats her students in very much the same way she is treated by her supervisors and colleagues. The climate of respect, openness, supportiveness, and participation that Starr experiences in her professional activities is the same climate that permeates her classroom. And it is this kind of climate that fosters language skills. As the district document "Language Arts Expectations" explains: "The environment for learning language is rich, filled with opportunity and invitation to speak, read, write, and listen. Students are immersed in language and literacy experiences that interest, engage, and challenge them."

Such an environment encourages students and teachers to be willing to experiment and take risks, and thus grow and learn. For example, as shown above, Starr's experiences with the research project and an NCTE workshop gave her the idea to try an inquiry-based approach for a student research project. After the project, she and the librarian could talk about the gains and losses resulting from such an approach. The school provides the kind of environment that encourages trying new approaches and reflecting on them. The result is that students are given new and better ways to learn and grow as well. As their philosophy statement suggests, "Hudson Middle School is an exciting learning community."

7 Creating the Educational Culture within Which Students Learn

As is demonstrated in the previous chapters, effective schools encourage their teachers to be active professionals who expect to keep up with knowledge and issues in the field and to participate in creating the kinds of changes that will make a difference in student learning. Effective teachers are in touch with their students, their profession, their colleagues, and society at large. And they use these differing contexts to gain knowledge and sensitivity to shape their curriculum, instruction, and assessment efforts in disciplinary and societally responsive ways that work for their students. The knowledge and experiences gained in their wide professional arena affect (directly or indirectly) the classroom context and their students' learning and achievement in at least three ways:

- Transported ideas: Ideas and activities with which they come into contact "fit" what the teachers in the proactive English programs have already been doing or searching for, and, when encountered, they are being used in a manner and in a classroom setting that are pedagogically compatible. Thus, although the activity may change over time, the initial theoretical "match" permits an easier try-on.

- Seed-bedded ideas: Ideas and activities interest teachers as potentially useful and are, as described by EIE researcher Eija Rougle, who identified and named this phenomenon, "put on the back burner" to be used in a variety of ways at some later time. These ideas are rarely used as initially presented but become part of an integrated programmatic or teacher-constructed approach, activity, or framework that in turn becomes part of the teacher's knowledge or action repertoire over time.

- Rejected ideas: Ideas and activities are rejected as falling outside the theoretical and pedagogical realm of what the teacher thinks is either useful or appropriate.

In all cases, the teacher never works in a vacuum, whether first engaging the ideas, discussing them, gathering feedback in understanding, reconstruing them, or even rejecting them. It is through constant exposure to and sifting through the broad and distant as well as the closer-to-home professional contexts that teachers maintain the professional knowledge, skills, and techniques they use to help their students learn and achieve in English. However, it is because they constantly air concerns and reactions to ideas in the professional arena in the ways described in this book that they are able to work through the centrifugal and centripetal forces and maintain common vision. This is how the successful programs gain their coherence yet remain open to constructive change.

Much call for educational reform has focused on changing the teacher, but this research suggests a need to change the setting—specifically, what Grossman, Valencia, Evans, Thompson, Martin, and Place (2000) call the activity setting. This setting includes the larger educational system within which decisions are made and goals are set that affect how teachers behave and grow as professionals, and thus how they create the educational culture within which students learn.

The educational culture described in this book was manifested in a number of ways. First, a history of cumulative reform efforts had been built upon others in the field and had created a school and district history of productive change (e.g., the Zelda Glazer Writing Project that built upon the Bay Area and National Writing Projects; efforts at Turner Tech and Highland Oaks that built upon the Coalition for Essential Schools; and efforts at International that built upon the Coalition and a number of other reform movements).

There was also a thorough and long-lived process of reculturing (Fullan & Hargreaves, 1991) that defined the interpersonal and professional environments of all the higher-performing schools, including Tawasentha in the nascent stages of moving toward changing its context. Furthermore, professional change and development were understood to require a reallocation of both monetary and time resources—although both were at times gained through external funding—and resources for a professional community were understood to involve collegiality, common goals, and joint activity that created a synergy that could make a difference.

These processes occurred within open rather than closed communities—open to new ideas from many places, and open to examination and discussion. Professional instructional features such as the ones discussed in this book were not easy to come by or enact; they resulted from the hard and ongoing work of dedicated professionals who permitted themselves to be both dreamers and doers. Neither is such a culture built quickly. Instead, it is built up over time, sustained by the willingness to persevere. It comes from an unremitting belief in public education, a belief that all students can learn, can have successful futures, and that it is in the power of the school to make it happen.

Are these things characteristic of all teachers in the departments in each of these schools, or only of special "lead teachers"? The schools described in this book "feel" good, from the moment you enter the doors. They are human places—places of learning, and also places of safety. They are exceptional educational environments because the overlapping features of the contexts invite them to be so. We cannot necessarily assume that any one of the teachers would have been wonderful (or at least as wonderful as they are) just anywhere. Instead, it is the array of features in the many contexts of their work lives that supports and feeds their excellence, and helps them sustain it. But not every teacher finds himself or herself in contexts as exceptionally rich and plentiful as the ones in which the various teachers in this study were situated. Nor does a rich context assure excellence. We all know there are teachers who burn out, who have other priorities, who resist participating in such rich contexts. But the mixture of educational features I have described—coordinating efforts to improve achievement, fostering teacher participation in professional communities, creating activities that allow teachers to exercise agency, valuing commitment to professionalism, engendering caring attitudes, and fostering respect for learning—seems to support more potentially exceptional teachers than usual, teachers who believe it is within their power to make a difference in their students' lives, and who thrive on making this a reality.

Time and again, when visiting these schools, we were impressed by the enthusiasm, knowledge, and dedication of the teachers and by the collaborative participation of the students in high-quality, "minds-on" activities. Although the schools felt and looked different from each other, and were organized very differently, certain noteworthy features consistently surrounded their students' experiences with English:

- effective English and literacy learning and instruction took place as separated and simulated as well as integrated experiences;
- test preparation was integrated into the ongoing instructional program;
- overt connections were constantly made across lessons, classes, and grades;
- students were taught strategies for thinking as well as doing;
- the goals of lessons involved generative thinking; and
- high literacy in English was treated as social activity.

These features, contextualized by example in the previous chapters, permeated the environments and provided marked distinctions between higher- and more typically performing schools.

These findings cut across high-poverty areas in inner cities as well as middle-class suburban communities. They obtained in schools that were scoring higher in English and literacy than other schools serving comparable populations of students. They involved concentrated efforts on the part of teachers to offer extremely well-conceived and well-delivered instruction based on identified goals about what is important to learn, and on an essential understanding of how the particular knowledge and skills identified as learning goals are used in carrying out real literacy activities. From these teachers, we have learned that it is not enough to teach to the test, to add additional tutoring sessions or mandated summer school classes, or to add test prep units or extra workbooks on grammar or literary concepts. While many forms of additional and targeted help were evident as parts of the effort to improve student achievement in the higher-performing schools, these alone were not enough. The overriding contributor to success was the whole-scale attention to students' higher literacy needs and development throughout the curriculum, which shaped what students experienced on a day-to-day basis in their regular classrooms. Such re-visioning of both curriculum and instruction requires a careful rethinking of the skills and knowledge that need to be learned, their integration for students' use in broader activities, and continued practice, discussion, and review of them as needed over time.

I hope these findings, and this book, provide us with a vision, a set of principles, and an array of examples to use as guides in re-visioning effective instruction.

Appendix A:
School Descriptions

ollowing is a brief description of each school that participated in the Excellence in English project. An asterisk denotes use of the school's actual name.

Florida (Miami-Dade County)

Highland Oaks Middle School* is located in a neighborhood of recent and rapid change. Of the full-time staff, 28 percent are African American and 13 percent Hispanic. With a 1,732-student enrollment, the school operates at 128 percent of capacity. Teachers and administrators are working extremely hard to maintain student achievement, even as the student body changes. Their effort is paying off. The students have scored above the statewide standard on the Florida Writes! Exam, with 80 percent scoring a 3 or higher. The state standard is 50 percent.

 Palm Middle School, built in the 1950s, is in a poor residential area. The school's mission is "to expose our students to technology-enriched learning experiences while providing a supportive, structured learning environment." The school has not thus far involved itself in districtwide curriculum and professional development efforts. Although there is extraordinary enthusiasm and administrative support for the prize-winning band and sports teams, this is less the case for academics. It is one of the lowest-performing middle schools in Dade County.

 Ruben Dario Middle School* serves a poor population; the school's poverty rate is one and a half times greater than the statewide average. It operates at 119 percent of capacity with 2,083 students, and its absentee rate is below the statewide average. Following district goals, it maintains a diverse full-time staff: 51 percent Hispanic, 23 percent Black non-Hispanic, and 21 percent White non-Hispanic. Although it was chartered as a Title I school in 1989, Ruben Dario's scores on the annual Florida Writes! Exam have steadily improved, with performance above the statewide standard. Florida's standard for grade 8 requires at least 50 percent of students to score a 3 or higher on a scale of 0 to 6. In 1997, 86 percent of Ruben Dario's students did so.

 Hendricks High School is in a federally designated empowerment zone that includes the largest public housing population in the area. The school, built in 1925, serves twenty-eight hundred students. Its sports program is well known, and many trophies line the halls. Hendricks is an International, Business and Finance Magnet School and is known for its arts and drafting program. There is also a Pivot Program for potential dropouts, and an active Junior ROTC program. All programs lead to an academic diploma. The Hendricks School Improvement Plan addresses the need for reading improvement and calls for implementation of the district's new curriculum, as well as staff development. It is one of the more typical schools in the study.

Miami Edison Senior High School* is the oldest school in the county, with a poor and transient student body. It is in a particularly high-crime portion of Miami. Thirty eight percent of the students are designated to receive free or reduced lunch. Serving 2,340 students, it operates at 116 percent of capacity. The school has a large, culturally diverse teaching staff. At the time of our study, Edison saw its general mission as providing students with alternatives for success; however, these were fragmented, offering little coherence at the school level. Although Edison had been identified by the district as low-performing, there was a move to change, and, as our study ended, the school underwent organizational restructuring through the institution of academies.

William H. Turner Technical Arts High School* is an alternative school of choice, with a student population of 2,119. It is a "two for one" school, offering a combined academic and vocational program whose goal is to prepare students to excel in their goals, be they in higher education or in the workforce. Turner Tech is a member of the Coalition of Essential Schools and seeks to develop the "habits of mind" advocated by Sizer (1992). Although there are no academic requirements for admission to the school, the attendance and academic standards are high; students are put on probation if they do not maintain good attendance and/or if they earn two or more Ds on a report card. In 1997, 90 percent of the students scored 3 or higher on the Florida Writes! Exam, with an average score of 3.6. Not only do Turner Tech's students continue to surpass state standards, but they are closing the gap with more middle-class schools in the state. In 1997, for example, 78 percent of the graduating class went on to some form of higher education.

New York

Abraham S. King Middle School is located on the outskirts of New York City and serves a diverse, high-poverty student population. Unlike most schools serving the urban poor, at King 89 percent of the students scored above the statewide reference point on an English language arts assessment, in comparison to 82 percent statewide. The school was recently named a Blue Ribbon School for helping students reach high standards. The district has a reputation for innovative programs to engage students and support higher performance. We studied the voluntary two-way bilingual program designed to help monolingual English-speaking students learn Spanish and their monolingual Spanish-speaking grademates learn English. Language proficiency is the goal across the curriculum. The program was initially funded by the state and has been held up as an example of innovative language instruction and high literacy achievement.

Crestwood Middle School is the lowest-performing middle school in its district. Crestwood's reading scores declined over time. Changes are under way to improve student achievement. The principal is new, as is one-third of the teaching staff. Overall, complaints among faculty are many and morale is low. School safety has been an issue, and security has been tightened. The out-of-school suspension rate is 38.5 percent, compared to a rate of 18 percent in similar schools.

Henry O. Hudson Middle School is in a middle-class community, a few miles outside of a medium-sized city. Its students consistently score above those at comparable schools and above the statewide norm. Although 90 percent of the student population is White, with no more than two or three students of color in each class, mainstreaming has added another kind of diversity, with special education and physically handicapped students in every classroom. Academic achievement is a high priority at Hudson, and teachers and administrators work collaboratively to maintain and extend excellence. Its teachers and administrators keep up with the latest research, discuss it based on their needs, and share what works. They remain active in their profession.

Stockton Middle School is situated in a once-middle-class, still-family-oriented neighborhood that has experienced a steady decline as resident-owned homes have been converted to rental property and crime has inched its way in. Stockton had been a high school until the early 1990s, when the district underwent a major reconfiguration to be more cost efficient and to achieve better integration across its student population. In recent years there has been a strong districtwide move to improve student achievement, with many new efforts under way at all levels. In turn, Stockton has been experiencing rising scores on state tests. Stockton also boasts the largest school orchestra in the district, exceeding even the high school. Musical events and a winning basketball team draw the community to the school on a consistent basis.

International High School* is a highly innovative school located in a busy commercial area of New York City. Although it is a school of choice, it is limited to students who have been in the United States for four years or less and have scores below the 21st percentile on the Language Assessment Battery. It offers a complete high school education through a content-based, English-as-a-second-language approach. In 1987, the 450-member student body came from forty-eight countries and spoke thirty-seven languages. Although the school does not administer the statewide achievement tests, it is known for its remarkable achievement record; more than 90 percent of its students go on to college, and this has been the case throughout its history. The school is affiliated with many educational reform projects that have high aspirations for students, including Opportunity to Learn, Center for Collaborative Education, Arts Connection, Coalition for Essential Schools, and New Visions for Public Schools.

New Westford High School is a small city high school in an area that has undergone population flight and economic change since the 1970s, due to industrial downsizing. The city is trying to redevelop its downtown area, and the school district, once one of the top city schools in the area, is trying to raise student performance. The administrative style had been top-down, and, at the time of our study, approaches to curriculum and instruction remained relatively unexamined. Attempts to move toward improvement had focused on literacy instruction in the primary grades and technology across the grades, with the possibility of building on New Westford's strength and making it a Fine Arts Magnet for the area. Despite the approaching prospect of a new English Regents Exam being instituted as of 1999, a test which must be passed by all students who wish to earn a high school diploma, little professional development or organizational or curricular rethinking had taken place.

Tawasentha High School is located at the outskirts of a small and poor industrial city that thrived at the turn of the twentieth century but then lost business, industry, and jobs as technology changed production. The district had been quite traditional, marked by low test scores and low goals. In response to a new and highly motivated superintendent of schools and a small but changing parent community, academic goals and hence instructional programs are changing. In the past, Tawasentha had consistently scored lower than comparable schools on the statewide tests. However, this had begun to change at the elementary level, the grades initially involved in major reform. When we began our study, such changes had not yet occurred at the high school, but were about to.

California

Foshay Learning Center* is a K–12 school that has undergone major reform. Before principal Howard Lapin took the helm, it had been a low-performing and run-down school. Within five years, it has attained national recognition as a successful learning environment. The entire school has an academic focus and has affiliated with the University of Southern California in a Neighborhood Academic Achievement Program, spearheaded by James Fleming, designed to offer an academically oriented college preparation program for students in the USC community. It is a New American School and an Urban Learning Center school, a model for transforming urban schools. We studied both the middle school and high school programs at Foshay.

Charles Drew Middle School is a sixty-year-old school with over two thousand students and a good reputation for student success and commitment to the school. It follows a school-based-management model and prides itself on being a friendly working community. It is part of a UCLA network; thus teachers are involved in ongoing professional interactions with the university.

Rita Dove Middle School is in an economically depressed area far from the city center. Although it follows the open walkway architectural style of many warm-weather localities, the school is fenced; even the food service is gated, and students' meals are served through a small opening. With 1,650 students, Dove is presently in state receivership based on low scores, which must be raised. The principal and teachers are anxious to raise scores; extra tutorial sessions before the regular school day and a variety of extra help for students and workshops for teachers have been put into place. One teacher participating in the study is a highly experienced master teacher whose students have consistently scored higher than their classmates. The second teacher is newer and motivated to excel.

Rutherford B. Hayes High School is a large, eighty-year-old, inner-city school of thirty-two hundred students in a high-poverty area. It is a school slated to go into receivership next year due to the numbers of students failing to pass the statewide exam; it must raise scores by 2 percent in order to continue its present administration and programming. It is a Math and Science Magnet and offers the Humanitas Program that integrates English and Social Studies with a focus on global cooperation.

    Springfield High School is an urban school with an enrollment of twenty-three hundred and a warm and friendly campus environment. It has a good reputation and strong community support. It has the backing of local agencies, including Creative Artists, and the students are engaged in many performing arts activities. It has a Foreign Language/International Studies Magnet and a Bilingual Business and Finance Academy, both of which offer college courses for credit. Springfield is a member of the UCLA collaborative, designed to enrich teachers' knowledge and students' abilities to enter college with greater preparation. A Saturday program offers development of job skills as well as opportunities for students to make up academic credit.

Texas

John H. Kirby Middle School, established in 1926, is located in a diverse neighborhood of older homes and local stores. An Annenberg Beacon School, it has repeatedly been rated "exemplary" in district accountability reviews. Its charter advances an academically strong and purposeful education, seeks similarly high results from all students, and serves as a model for effective school reform and systemic change. To accomplish this goal, it established a school-based center for research and development of best practices. Its Vanguard program offers an accelerated and enriched curriculum, and it ranks 58 percent of its students as potentially gifted or talented. The school cultivates a sense of community through Cooperative Discipline, which emphasizes courtesies and expectations.

    Parklane Middle School is located in a thriving business district of a large city. It is adjacent to middle-class and affluent residential areas and also serves students from nearby poorer communities. It is a neighborhood school with a strong PTO that sponsors professional development activities. Parklane has a strong focus on literacy learning, and the students consistently perform well on state and other assessments.

    Ruby Middle School is one of the poorest and lowest-performing schools in its inner-city district. Before the present principal was hired, Ruby was a "battleground for crime." Teacher morale and cooperation was and still is low. In 1995, a consortium was formed by Ruby and nearby Lincoln High School to initiate a school improvement plan. The school has been making efforts to help families become involved in their children's education. Student behavior has been improving, and test scores have been slowly rising.

    Lincoln High School is located in a high-poverty community on the outskirts of a large city. Although it draws students from the same neighborhood as Ruby Middle School, its students have performed consistently well on statewide high-stakes assessments. Lincoln has an ROTC and Aviation Sciences magnet program. Teachers are encouraged to engage in professional development, try new ideas, and collaborate. Departments meet weekly for planning and coordination, as do grade-level-based group. Strict discipline is maintained. The students are well behaved and participate in many extra curricular activities. A Saturday academy provides tutorial help. The principal and staff have maintained good relations with the local community, and local police readily help keep the school safe.

Lyndon B. Johnson High School, a community school with a diverse student population, has a reputation for good teachers and solid performance. It offers an International Baccalaureate Program for advanced academics and a magnet program in research and technology. It offers many after-school clubs, organizations, and programs and has award-winning bands. Focused on improving its upper-level academic offerings and increasing the numbers of students in those programs, it aims to double the number of college-bound students to 80 percent.

Sam Rayburn High School, a comprehensive high school of two thousand students, has recently begun showing improvement after years of being rated low-performing by the state. Seventy percent of the students are deemed at-risk, because they either failed a course or were retained. Traditionally, Rayburn has prepared more students for the workplace than for college. It offers an extensive career and technology program, and the facilities house welding, machine, and carpentry shops. Business and health science career preparation are also offered. About 20 percent of the student body is presently enrolled in the Computer Technology Magnet program, the principal college-preparation offering. Rayburn has been chosen for participation in the Annenberg Challenge Reform Initiative, supporting its efforts to engage in experimentation, innovation, and change, with the goal of increased performance.

Appendix B: Related Reports from the Excellence in English Project

The following reports are published by and available from the National Research Center on English Learning & Achievement, University at Albany, State University of New York: http://cela.albany.edu.

Bonissone, Paola. (2000). *Teaming to Teach English to International High School Students: A Case Study.* Report No. 13005.

Confer, Carla. (1999). *Interactions between Central Office Language Arts Administrators and Exemplary English Teachers, and the Impact on Student Performance.* Report No. 12003.

Cruz, Gladys. (2000). *Collegial Networks: A Team of Sixth-Grade Teachers in a Two-Way Bilingual Program.* Report No. 13008.

Helmar-Salasoo, Ester, with Kahr, Sally. (1999). *Collegial Support and Networks Invigorate Teaching: The Case of Marsha S. Slater.* Report No. 12008.

Langer, Judith A. (1999). *Excellence in English in Middle and High School: How Teachers' Professional Lives Support Student Achievement.* Report No. 12002. (Also appeared in *American Educational Research Journal, 37*(2), 397–439: Summer 2000.).

Langer, Judith A. (2000). *Beating the Odds: Teaching Middle and High School Students to Read and Write Well.* 2nd edition. Report No. 12014. (Also appeared in *American Educational Research Journal, 38*(4), 837–880: Winter 2001.

Langer, Judith A., with Close, Elizabeth, Angelis, Janet, and Preller, Paula. (2000). *Guidelines for Teaching Middle and High School Students to Read and Write Well.*

Manning, Tanya. (2000). *Achieving High Quality Reading and Writing in an Urban Middle School: The Case of Gail Slatko.* Report No. 13001.

Ostrowski, Steven. (1999). *Vocational School Teacher Engages Students in High Level Reading and Writing: The Case of Janas Masztal.* Report No. 12006.

Ostrowski, Steven. (2000). *How English Is Taught and Learned in Four Exemplary Middle and High School Classrooms.* Report No. 13002.

Rougle, Eija. (1999). *A Middle School Teacher Never Stops Learning: The Case of Cathy Starr.* Report No. 12005.

Snyder, Sallie. (1999). *Beating the Odds over Time: One District's Perspective.* Report No. 12004.

Appendix C: Effective English Instruction—Tables

Table 1. Approaches to Skills Instruction

	Percentage of Teachers		
Dominant Approach	Effective Teachers in Effective Schools (N=26)*	Effective Teachers in Typical Schools (N=6)	Typical Teachers in Typical Schools (N=12)
Separated			50%
Simulated			17%
Integrated	27%	33%	17%
All Three	73%	67%	17%

*N denotes number of teachers in a given category.

Table 2. Approaches to Test Preparation

	Percentage of Teachers		
Dominant Approach	Effective Teachers in Effective Schools (N=26)*	Effective Teachers in Typical Schools (N=6)	Typical Teachers in Typical Schools (N=12)
Integrated	85%	83%	
Separated			75%
Both	15%	17%	8%
None			17%

*N denotes number of teachers in a given category.

Table 3. Connecting Learnings

Dominant Approach	Percentage of Teachers		
	Effective Teachers in Effective Schools (N=26)*	Effective Teachers in Typical Schools (N=6)	Typical Teachers in Typical Schools (N=12)
Within lessons			17%
Across lessons	12%		
In and out of school			25%
All three connections	88%	100%	
No connections			58%

*N denotes number of teachers in a given category.

Table 4. Enabling Strategies

Dominant Approach	Percentage of Teachers		
	Effective Teachers in Effective Schools (N=26)*	Effective Teachers in Typical Schools (N=6)	Typical Teachers in Typical Schools (N=12)
Overtly taught	100%	100%	17%
Left implicit			83%

*N denotes number of teachers in a given category.

Table 5. Conceptions of Learning

Dominant Approach	Percentage of Teachers		
	Effective Teachers in Effective Schools (N=26)*	Effective Teachers in Typical Schools (N=6)	Typical Teachers in Typical Schools (N=12)
Focus on immediate goal			100%
Focus on deeper understanding	100%	100%	

*N denotes number of teachers in a given category.

Table 6. Classroom Organization

Dominant Approach	Percentage of Teachers		
	Effective Teachers in Effective Schools (N=26)*	Effective Teachers in Typical Schools (N=6)	Typical Teachers in Typical Schools (N=12)
Shared cognition	96%	100%	8%
Individual thinking	4%		92%

*N denotes number of teachers in a given category.

Appendix D: Activity Guide for the Motion Team at International High School

"To Build a Fire" by Jack London

Name _____

Group Members: _____

_____

_____

Credit earned: _____

"The more you move, the longer you live." Discuss with your group and decide what you think this sentence means about people physically and mentally. Each person should write the answers in his or her own words.

Physically:

Mentally:

Before you begin to read, here is some vocabulary you will need to know. Discuss the words and write down their meanings. Use a dictionary only if no one in the group knows the meanings.

Yukon
spat—past of spit
frostbite
numb
thaw out
chuckled
whiplashes
moccasins

BEFORE YOU READ THE STORY, READ ALL THE DIRECTIONS BELOW:

Imagine you are in one of the coldest places in the world and are going on a trip. There are no cars, planes, or trains. How will you get from one place to another?

What dangers are there?

What would you need to survive?

Now you are ready to read. If you have a problem as you read, ask for help. You may need to read this story more than once. Everyone will have to take the story home to reread or finish so you can do the following work together in class. Look at how many pages there are. When will everyone finish this story? Decide together and write it below:

We will finish the story by_____.

When you finish reading the whole story, do the following:

Write down all the questions you have about the story or any parts that confuse you. Use the space below to write your questions.

Discuss your questions with your group and write the answers. Use this space.

Now answer these questions:

What happens in the story? Write a *short* plot summary of five to six sentences that includes the beginning, the middle, and the end.

How do you feel about the end? Would you change it? How?

The **conflict** of a story is a struggle between an important character and another person or thing or force. One side wins. What is the conflict in this story?

Who wins it?

Is this inevitable (unavoidable)? Why or why not?

By having the conflict end this way, what do you think Jack London is saying about life? That is, what is the **theme** of this story?

We can see how physical motion is important in this story. The character also moves mentally. How does the journey change his view of life? If you can, use lines from the story to support your ideas.

How does this change affect the way you feel about him?

Discuss as a group and write a paragraph answering the following question:

What is the relationship between movement and change? In your paragraph, relate this to any work on movement and change you did in physics/math or Project Adventure. Each person should write the paragraph in his or her own words.

Mastery Questions
If you need more space, attach additional sheets of paper.

Why do you think the man ignores the danger and goes on his journey anyway? What do you think this says about people? Do you agree or disagree? Explain your answer. Give reasons. Try to find reasons that you can back up with lines from the story.

In the story, the author, Jack London, shows us the dog's thoughts as well as the man's thoughts. How is the way the man thinks different from the way the dog thinks? Why do you think this is so? What do you think London is showing us about the difference between people and animals? What evidence from the story makes you think this? Do you agree or disagree? Explain your answer. Give reasons.

In the ending of the story, the man keeps moving, hoping it will help, even though he is pretty sure it will not. Why do you think he continues to move anyway? That is, what is it about moving that is important to human beings? What evidence do you have from the story or your personal experience that this is so? That is, why do you think this?

Think about the saying you already discussed before reading the story: "The more you move, the longer you live." Do you see any more meanings in it now, after you have read the story? What new meanings do you see about people physically and mentally? What are your reasons?

Notes

Chapter 1

1. See Appendix A for a brief description of each of the twenty-five schools and Appendix B for a list of our published reports on those schools.

2. The studies have also been presented in the *American Educational Research Journal* (Langer, 2000, 2001).

Chapter 2

1. To read about how other effective teachers use a variety of approaches to skills instruction, see Chapter 4, specifically the section beginning on page 86, "Teaching and Learning Mechanics and Vocabulary," and Chapter 5, specifically the section beginning on page 128, "Mechanics and Grammar."

2. To read more examples of effective teachers making connections within and across lessons and across in-school and out-of-school applications, see Chapter 4, specifically the section beginning on page 78, "Teaching and Learning Writing," and Chapter 6, specifically the segment in the section "'Lots of Writing'" that addresses connecting art and poetry (page 152).

3. To read about how Cathy Starr teaches reading strategies, see Chapter 6, specifically the section beginning on page 151, "'Lots of Reading.'"

4. To read more specifics about how Slater's students worked in groups, see Chapter 5, specifically the section beginning on page 121, "Student Talk."

5. To read more about group work in Starr's classroom, see Chapter 6, in the section beginning on page 155, "'Lots of Discussion, Lots of Student Questions.'"

6. For more examples of these dynamic learning communities in action, see Chapter 4, in the sections beginning on pages 89 and 97, "Teaching and Learning Literature" and "English and the Uses of Oral Language," respectively.

Chapter 3

1. To read more about the peer evaluations at International, see Chapter 5, especially the section "Peer Support and Peer Evaluation Teams," beginning on page 104, and the section "Reflection and Evaluation in Slater's Professional Experience," beginning on page 112.

2. To read about Starr's involvement in professional organizations, see Chapter 6, specifically the section beginning on page 145, "Professional Associations."

3. To read more about Gold and Gropper, see Chapter 4.

4. You can read more about Kirchner and colleagues in Chapter 4.

5. To read about one teacher's sense of agency at International High School, see Chapter 5, specifically the section beginning on page 134, "Links between Slater's Professional Life and Her Classroom Practice."

6. To read more about Starr's commitment to professionalism, see Chapter 6, specifically the section beginning on page 140, "Starr's Professional Life."

7. To read a discussion on the caring environment evident in four teachers' classrooms, see Chapter 4, specifically the section beginning on page 75, "Classroom Dynamics and Intimacy." Also see the section "The Relationship between Starr's Professional Life and the Way Language Arts Is Taught and Learned in Her Classroom," which begins on page 159 in Chapter 6.

Chapter 4

1. The Coalition of Essential Schools (CES), founded in 1985, is a national network of schools, support centers, and a national office engaged in restructuring schools to promote better student learning and achievement.

2. School-within-a-school organization creates a smaller and often a more focused community for students. Students and teachers can get to know one another better. These groups often have their own principal and staff, and they can be focused on a specific topic or theme or arranged by grade.

Works Cited

Adler, M., & Flihan, S. (1997). *The interdisciplinary continuum: Reconciling theory, research and practice.* (Report Series 10004). Albany, NY: National Research Center on English Learning & Achievement, University at Albany, State University of New York.

Applebee, A. N. (1993). *Literature in the secondary school: Studies of curriculum in the United States.* Urbana, IL: National Council of Teachers of English.

Applebee, A. N. (1996). *Curriculum as conversation: Transforming traditions of teaching and learning.* Chicago: University of Chicago Press.

Arreaga-Mayer, C., & Perdomo-Rivera, C. (1996). Ecobehavioral analysis of instruction for at-risk language-minority students. *The Elementary School Journal, 96*(3), 245–258.

Bakhtin, M. M. (1981). *The dialogic imagination.* (C. Emerson & M. Holquist, Trans.). Austin, TX: University of Texas Press.

Barnes, D. (1976). *From communication to curriculum.* London: Penguin.

Bazerman, C. (1981). What written knowledge does: Three examples of academic discourse. *Philosophy of the Social Sciences, 11*(3), 361–387.

Bereiter, C., & Scardamalia, M. (1987). An attainable version of high literacy: Approaches to teaching higher-order skills in reading and writing. *Curriculum Inquiry, 17*(1), 9–30.

Bloom, B. S. (1971). Mastery learning and its implications for curriculum development. In E. W. Eisner (Ed.), *Confronting curriculum reform* (pp. 17–49). Boston: Little, Brown.

Bransford, J. D., Brown, A. L., & Cocking, R. R. (Eds.). (1999). *How people learn: Brain, mind, experience, and school.* Washington, DC: National Academy Press.

Brown, A. L., & Campione, J. (1996). Psychological theory and the design of innovative learning environments: On procedures, principles, and systems. In L. Schauble & R. Glaser (Eds.), *Innovations in learning: New environments for education* (pp. 289–325). Mahwah, NJ: Erlbaum.

Cohen, D. K. (1995). What is the system in systemic reform? *Educational Researcher, 24*(9), 11–17.

Cope, B., & Kalantzis, M. (1993). The power of literacy and the literacy of power. In B. Cope & M. Kalantzis (Eds.), *The powers of literacy: A genre approach to teaching writing* (pp. 154–178). Pittsburgh: University of Pittsburgh Press.

Dewey, J. (1938). *Experience and education.* New York: Collier.

Elbow, P. (1973). *Writing without teachers.* New York: Oxford University Press.

Elley, W. B. (1997). *In praise of incidental learning: Lessons from some empirical findings on language acquisition.* (Report Series 10002). Albany, NY:

National Research Center on English Learning & Achievement, University at Albany, State University of New York.

Fiske, E. B., with Reed, S., & Sautter, R. C. (1991). *Smart schools, smart kids: Why do some schools work?* New York: Simon & Schuster.

Fullan, M., & Hargreaves, A. (1991). *What's worth fighting for? Working together for your school.* Andover, MA: Regional Laboratory for Educational Improvement of the Northeast and Islands in association with Ontario Public School Teachers' Federation; and Washington, DC: U.S. Department of Education, Office of Educational Research and Improvement.

Goodman, Y. M., & Wilde, S. (Eds.). (1992). *Literacy events in a community of young writers.* Language and Literacy Series. New York: Teachers College Press.

Graff, G. (1987). *Professing literature: An institutional history.* Chicago: University of Chicago Press.

Graves, D. H. (1983). *Writing: Teachers and children at work.* Exeter, NH: Heinemann.

Grossman, P., Valencia, S., Evans, K., Thompson, C., Martin, S., & Place, N. (2000). *Transitions into teaching: Learning to teach writing in teacher education and beyond.* Research report No. 13006. Albany, NY: National Research Center on English Learning & Achievement, University at Albany, State University of New York.

Guthrie, J. T., & Alvermann, D. E. (Eds.). (1999). *Engaged reading: Processes, practices, and policy implications.* New York: Teachers College Press.

Hillocks, G., Jr. (1995). *Teaching writing as reflective practice.* New York: Teachers College Press.

Hirsch, E. D., Jr. (1996). *The schools we need and why we don't have them.* New York: Doubleday.

Langer, J. A. (1992). *Critical thinking and English language arts instruction.* (Report Series 6.5). Albany, NY: National Research Center on Literature Teaching and Learning, University at Albany, State University of New York.

Langer, J. A. (1995). *Envisioning literature: Literary understanding and literature instruction.* New York: Teachers College Press.

Langer, J. A. (2000). Excellence in English in middle and high school: How teachers' professional lives support student achievement. *American Educational Research Journal, 37*(2), 397–439. (Also CELA Report Series 12002).

Langer, J. A. (2001). Beating the odds: Teaching middle and high school students to read and write well. *American Educational Research Journal, 38*(4), 837–880. (Also CELA Report Series 12014).

Langer, J. A., & Allington, R. L. (1992). Curriculum research in writing and reading. In P. W. Jackson (Ed.), *Handbook of research on curriculum: A project of the American Educational Research Association* (pp. 687–725). New York: MacMillan.

Langer, J. A., & Applebee, A. N. (1987). *How writing shapes thinking: A study of teaching and learning.* Urbana, IL: National Council of Teachers of English.

Louis, K. S., Marks, H. M., & Kruse, S. (1996). Teachers' professional community in restructuring schools. *American Educational Research Journal, 33*(4), 757–798.

McLaughlin, M. W., & Talbert, J. E. (1993). *Contexts that matter for teaching and learning: Strategic opportunities for meeting the nation's education goals.* Stanford, CA: Center for Research on the Context of Secondary School Teaching, Stanford University.

Myers, M. (1996). *Changing our minds: Negotiating English and literacy.* Urbana, IL: National Council of Teachers of English.

National Assessment of Educational Progress (NAEP). (1998). National Writing Summary Data Tables for Grade 8 Teacher Data. Available online at http://www.nces.ed.gov/nationsreportcard/naepdata/qtoc.asp. (Accessed March 11, 2002).

Noddings, N. (1984). *Caring: A feminine approach to ethics and moral education.* Berkeley: University of California Press.

Nystrand, M., with Gamoran, A., Kachur, R., & Prendergast, C. (1997). *Opening dialogue: Understanding the dynamics of language and learning in the English classroom.* (Language and Literacy Series). New York: Teachers College Press.

Nystrand, M., Gamoran, A., & Carbonaro, W. (1998). *Towards an ecology of learning: The case of classroom discourse and its effects on writing in high school English and social studies.* (Report Series 11001). Albany, NY: National Research Center on English Learning & Achievement, University at Albany, State University of New York.

Nystrand, M., Gamoran, A., & Heck, M. J. (1993). Using small groups for response to and thinking about literature. *English Journal, 82*(1), 14–22.

Ostrowski, S. (1999). *Vocational school English teacher engages students in high levels of reading and writing: The case of Janas Masztal.* (Report Series 12006). Albany, NY: National Research Center on English Learning & Achievement, University at Albany, State University of New York.

Page, S. (1997, October 13). USA's most diverse neighborhood. *USA Today.*

Paris, S. G., Wasik, G. A., & Turner, J. C. (1991). The development of strategic readers. In R. Barr, M. L. Kamil, P. Mosenthal, & P. D. Pearson (Eds.), *Handbook of reading research.* Volume II. New York: Longman.

Pressley, M., El-Dinary, P. B., Brown, R., Schuder, T. L., Pioli, M., Green, K., & Gaskins, I. (1994). Transactional instruction of comprehension strategies: The Montgomery County, Maryland, SAIL Program. *Reading and Writing Quarterly, 10*(1), 5–19.

Raphael, T. E., & McMahon, S. I. (1994). Book club: An alternative framework for reading instruction. *The Reading Teacher, 48*(2), 102–116.

Rogoff, B. (1994). Developing understanding of the idea of community of learners. *Mind, Culture and Activity, 1,* 209–229.

Rosenblatt, L. M. (1978). *The reader, the text, the poem: The transactional theory of the literary work.* Carbondale, IL: Southern Illinois University Press.

Saphier, J., and King, M. (1985). Good seeds grow in strong cultures. *Educational Leadership, 42*(6), 67–74.

Schallert, D. L. (1976). Improving memory for prose: The relationship between depth of processing and context. *Journal of Verbal Learning and Verbal Behavior, 15,* 621–632.

Sizer, T. R. (1984). *Horace's Compromise: The Dilemma of the American High School.* Boston: Houghton Mifflin.

Slavin, R. E., Madden, N. A., Dolan, L. J., Wasik, B. A., Ross, W., Smith, L., & Dianda, M. (1996). Success for all: A summary of research. *Journal of Education for Students Placed at Risk, 1*(1), 41–76.

Smith, M. S., & O'Day, J. (1991). Systemic school reform. In S. H. Fuhrman & B. Malem (Eds.), *The politics of curriculum and testing: The 1990 Yearbook of the Politics of Education Association.* London: Falmer.

Toulmin, S. (1958). *The uses of argument.* Cambridge, UK: Cambridge University Press.

Vygotsky, L. S. (1978). *Mind in society: The development of higher psychological processes.* Cambridge, MA: Harvard University Press.

Index

text, marking of, 151
thinking, teaching of, 131
"To Build a Fire" (London), 121, 177–81
To Kill a Mockingbird (Lee), 34
Toulmin, S., 82
transmission teaching, 111
Turner, Evangeline, 20, 31
tutors,
    peer, 108–9
    teachers as, 139

"Unicorn in the Garden, The" (Thurber),
    130

vocabulary, teaching of, 88–89
voice,
    development of, 123–24
    power of, 124
Vygotsky, Lev, 34, 118, 131

"Wake of the Ferry II" (Sloan), 154
warrants, 82

Weiss, Margaret, 44, 58, 59
    on teacher as agent, 55
Wilde, Sandra, 12
William H. Turner Technical Arts High
    School, 55
    demographics of, 5
    description of, 67, 166
World Wide Web, use of, 62
writing,
    poetry, 153–54
    as recursive activity, 81
    rubrics, 145
    teaching of, 78–86, 126–29, 152–55
writing exercises, 84
writing process, 126
writing prompts, 29–31, 153
writing theory, 111

Yearling, The (Rawlings), 54

Zelda Glazer/Dade County Writing
    Project, 4
zones of proximal development, 131

Author

Judith A. Langer is distinguished professor at the University at Albany, State University of New York, and director of the National Research Center on English Learning & Achievement (CELA). Her studies of language, literacy, and learning have had a major impact on English and literacy theory, teaching, and assessment.

Langer serves on many advisory boards and national reform groups involved in rethinking literacy education. Her major works examine the nature of literate thought—the knowledge students use when they "make sense" and the ways in which their learning is affected by activities and interactions in the classroom. After studying the professional and classroom features of English programs where students are "beating the odds" in literacy achievement, she has focused her most recent research scholarship on the kinds of professional and instructional activities that need to be put in place to improve student learning.

Langer's many articles have been published in a wide variety of journals and collections. Her books include *Reader Meets Author/Bridging the Gap: A Psycholinguistic and Sociolinguistic Perspective* (with M. Trika Smith-Burke); *Understanding Reading and Writing Research* (with Michael L. Kamil and Timothy Shanahan); *Children Reading and Writing: Structures and Strategies; Language, Literacy, and Culture: Issues of Society and Schooling; How Writing Shapes Thinking: A Study of Teaching and Learning* (with Arthur N. Applebee); *Literature Instruction: A Focus on Student Response; Literature Instruction: Practice and Policy* (with James Flood); and *Envisioning Literature: Literary Understanding and Literature Instruction.*

Contributors

Paola R. Bonissone is a doctoral candidate in curriculum and instruction at the University at Albany. Her research interests include literacy instructional practices for adult English language learners as well as how differing practices affect literacy and language learning.

Sally Jo Bronner is the director of training programs at the Institute for Cultural Partnerships, Harrisburg, Pennsylvania. She has served as an educational consultant to the State Museum of Pennsylvania. She led the Anti-Defamation League's national anti-bias campaign in Boston. She was a founding faculty member of Brooklyn International High School, and was adjunct professor of developmental speech at Touro College in New York City. She received her B.A. in English from Hebrew University, Jerusalem, and earned her M.S. in teaching English as a second language and studied in the doctoral program in language in education at the University at Albany, State University of New York.

Ester Helmar-Salasoo received her Ph.D. from the University at Albany and is presently a researcher at the National Research Center on English Learning & Achievement. She completed her bachelor of arts degree and graduate diploma in education at the University of Western Australia, as well as TESL training in England, and a master of science (TESOL) degree at the University at Albany, State University of New York. She has taught English, literature, humanities, and ESL for ten years in high schools in Western Australia and has taught in the Intensive English Language Program at the University at Albany. She began her own schooling not speaking English, and uses Estonian as the home language with her husband and three children in upstate New York.

Steven D. Ostrowski currently teaches in the English department at Central Connecticut State University, where he directs the English education program. His research and scholarly interests include the teaching and learning of writing and literature, and the relationship between religious faith and literary art. In addition to literacy-related research, he has published fiction and poetry in numerous literary reviews and journals.

Eija Rougle is a doctoral candidate at the University at Albany, State University of New York, and is an instructional facilitator at the National Research Center on English Learning & Achievement. She taught language arts for many years in Sweden and published an award-winning primer for minority students in Sweden. She has extensive experience in American classrooms, especially at the middle school level, through research collaborations under the auspices of the National Research Center on English Learning & Achievement. Her work has been published in Scandinavia and in the United States. Her research interests are English language arts pedagogy, literacy learning within social contexts, and development of literary understanding within dialogic discourse(s).

This book was typeset in Palatino and Helvetica by Precision Graphics.
The typefaces used on the cover were Slimbach and Chaparral Display.
The book was printed on 50-lb. Williamsburg Offset by Versa Press, Inc.